ETWATER

Technical Institute

TSTIWACO

Texas State Technical Institute

TSTISYSTEM

Texas State Technical Institute

STC

tate
College™

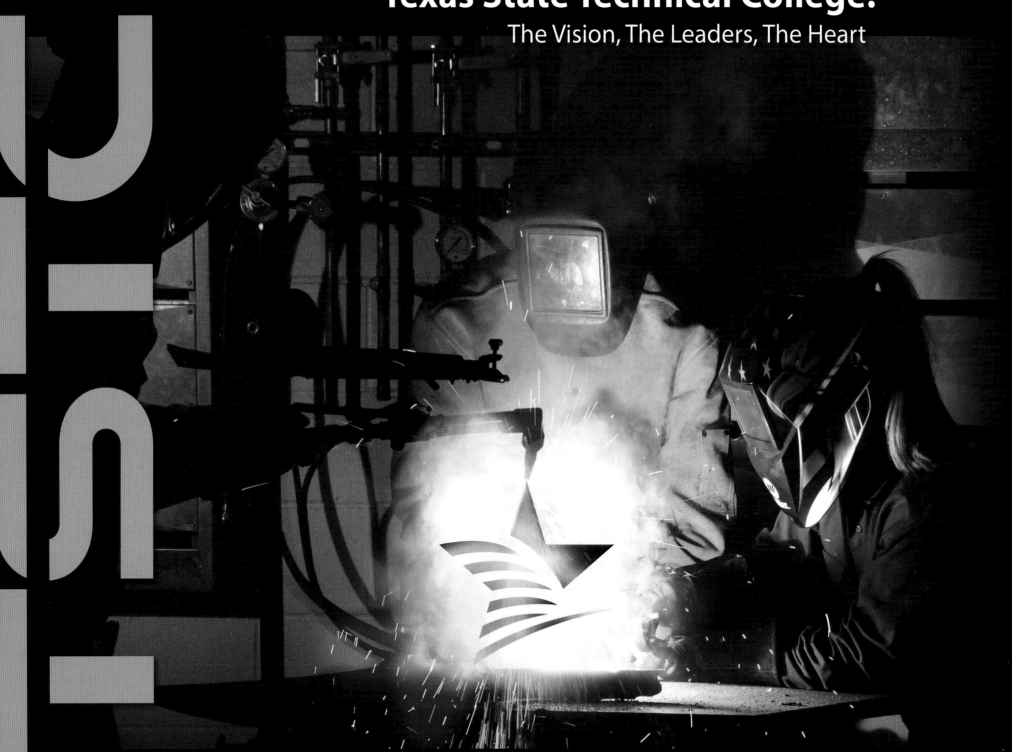

Texas State Technical College:
The Vision, The Leaders, The Heart

50 Years of Changing Lives and Building Texas, 1965–2015

By Marlene S. McMichael

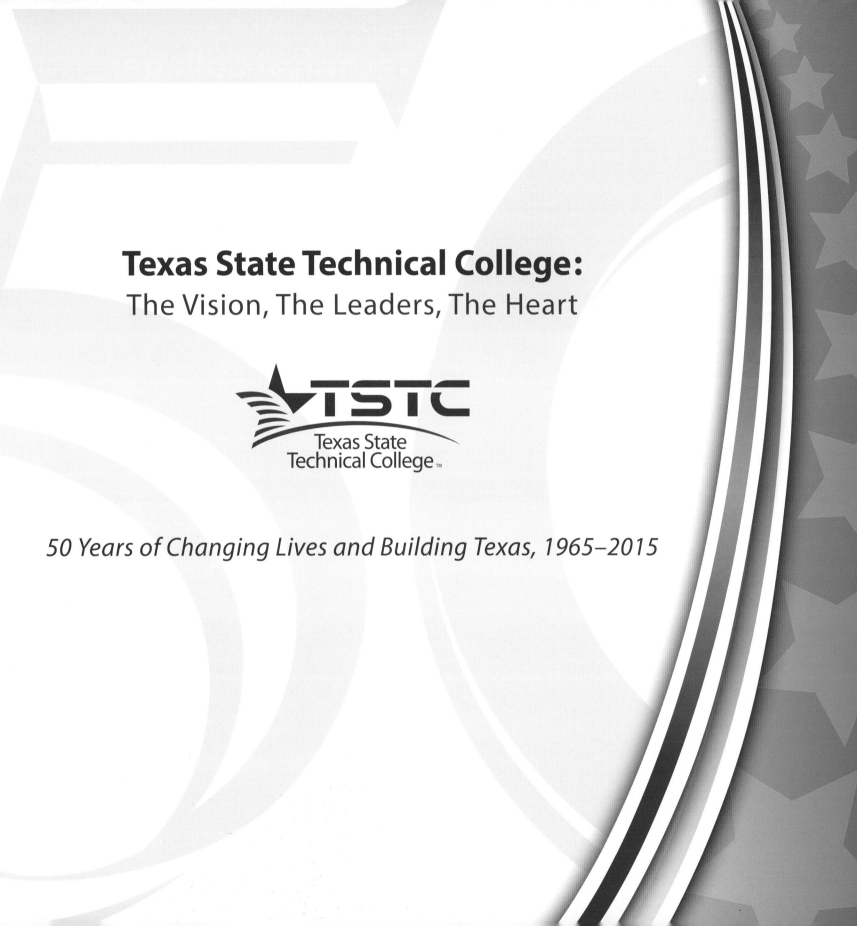

Texas State Technical College:

The Vision, The Leaders, The Heart

TSTC
Texas State
Technical College™

50 Years of Changing Lives and Building Texas, 1965–2015

Dear Reader:

Welcome! We're happy to present you with the first fifty years of Texas State Technical College (TSTC), and we're sure you'll find some interesting reading in these pages.

We've all heard the saying, "Education is its own reward;" but, at TSTC, we think the intrinsic reward of college is just part of the picture. Indeed, a good education does more than enrich the heart and mind. It develops the knowledge and skills that will optimize the employability of students. After all, in today's Texas, a good job is an essential early step toward a life of fulfilling citizenship.

This notion of a dual-purpose education is not really new. It was fifty years ago when Texas conceived of a place where students could go to earn both job-essential skills and an expanded horizon. TSTC was and is that place, and this book is a celebration of our first five decades.

While the pace of change in technology continues to accelerate and re-shape how we do things, one thing will not change: TSTC remains a place where competent, committed, and caring people serve students who are hopeful, ambitious, and energetic. Best of all, by way of our worthy work and study together, all are rewarded.

Looking to the next fifty years,

Michael L. Reeser
Chancellor
Texas State Technical College

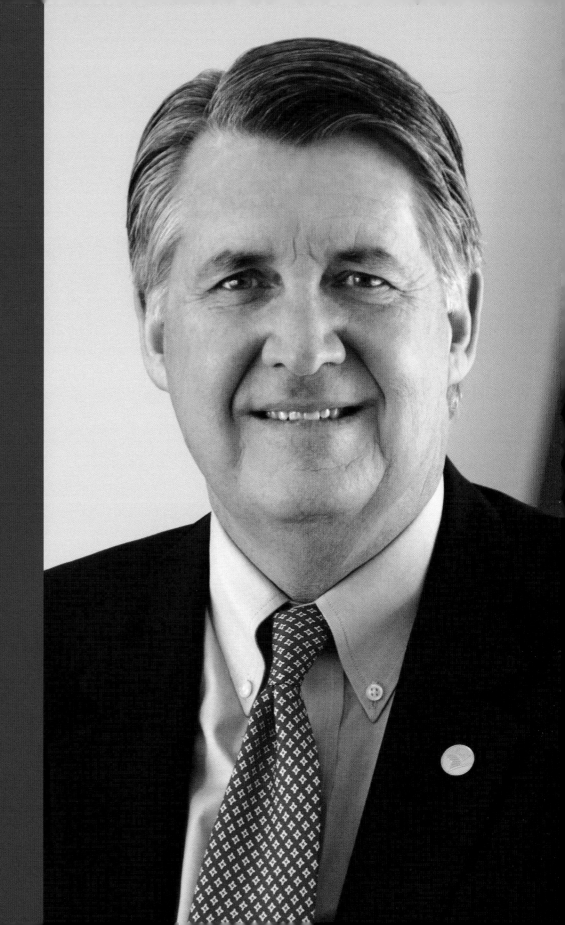

Acknowledgments

This book would have never come together without the encouragement, patience, and diligent work of the project manager for the 50th Anniversary Celebration, Julie Threlkeld, who spent untold hours combing through dusty archives, managing schedules, and ensuring an on-time delivery. Julie has become more than colleague and collaborator; she has become a friend.

There were many across the various campuses which make up Texas State Technical College (TSTC) who collected information or checked facts. In every case, my requests for help meant additional work for the person involved. While there are too many to name, please know I am sincerely grateful.

Many thanks are also due to the administrators, instructors, and students (both past and present) who submitted to interviews and freely shared their reflections. Without their stories, this book would have simply been a collection of dates and facts. They brought "heart" to the TSTC story.

Lastly, I extend a very special thank-you to Chancellor Michael L. Reeser, the leadership team, and Vice Chancellor Roger Miller who wanted this book to happen and who gave me the freedom to see it through to publication.

Artifact Contributors:

Daily Photography
Deborah Sanders
Mario Cantu
Elaine Frazier
Benjamin Cantu
Mark Burdine
Betty Dupree
Maria Aguirre
Maria Lopez
National WASP WWII Museum
Gary Hendricks
Bill Clark
Nikki L. Gonzales
Gail Lawrence
TSTC Library Archives
Adam McGrath
Karen Sonnenberg
Melissa Curtis
Heather Karl
Harlingen Arts and Heritage Museum
Valley Morning Star
Learning Resource Center
Nancy Hendrick
Daisy Castillo
Deborah Coleman
Anita Knight
Gwen Kirby
Rene Ralston
Jose "Lupe" Navarrette

50th Anniversary Governance Committee:

Maria Aguirre
Jan Osburn
Valeri Smith
Carliss Hyde
Edgar Padilla
Baily Atchley
Benji Cantu
Julie Cromeens
Nick Alvarado
Dora Colvin
Lynda Lopez
Belinda Palomino
Amy Lynch
Shelli Scherwitz
Kelly Contella
Eliska Smith
Julie Threlkeld
Marlene S. McMichael

From the Author

After reviewing piles of old documents and photos, volumes of both oral and written histories, and dozens of web-based articles, it became clear that a listing of facts and dates could never tell the story of Texas State Technical College (TSTC). Facts are, of course, important. We are a technical college, after all.

TSTC's real story reaches beyond the telling of what happened on a specific date. It is, instead, revealed in the lives of people who dared to dream, to fight for a vision, to change their life's course, and to chart a new path—all to make a difference in their lives and in the lives of others.

The most inspiring part of my research was the realization that these "difference makers" were not limited to politicians, VIPs, or administrators. They included community leaders, instructors, and students. Governor John B. Connally was the "difference maker" who wanted Texas to have "the most sophisticated technical vocational training institute in the country," and Dr. Roy W. Dugger was the administrator who was tasked with working around a myriad of obstacles to make it happen. These are recognizable names, but "difference makers" also included any of the thousands of students who were the first in their families to step tentatively into a college-level classroom. These students changed lives, too. They began by changing their own.

While fifty years of facts are definitely included in this book, so is a tiny sampling of the stories of the amazing individuals who wove the fabric of TSTC's history. They are visionaries who worked to change lives for the better. They are all "difference makers." Together, they are TSTC.

TSTC gives students the skills and pathways to succeed in real-world jobs—jobs which support families and which are the backbone of Texas industry. Governor Connally would be pleased to know TSTC is still changing lives, and no other institution in technical education does it better.

Marlene S. McMichael, CPM
Associate Vice Chancellor for Government Affairs
Texas State Technical College

The Donning Company Publishers
184 Business Park Drive, Suite 206
Virginia Beach, VA 23462

Lex Cavanah, General Manager
Barbara Buchanan, Office Manager
Anne Burns, Editor
Jeremy Glanville, Graphic Designer
Monika Ebertz, Imaging Artist
Kathy Snowden Railey, Project Research Coordinator
Nathan Stufflebean, Research and Marketing Supervisor
Katie Gardner, Marketing Advisor

Jim Railey, Project Director

Library of Congress Cataloging-in-Publication Data

McMichael, Marlene S.
   Texas State Technical College : the vision, the leaders, the heart : 50 years of changing lives and building Texas, 1965-2015 / by Marlene S. McMichael.
      pages cm
   Includes bibliographical references.
   ISBN 978-1-57864-944-0
1. Texas State Technical College System–History. 2. Technical education–Texas–History. I. Title.
   T171.T3324M35 2014
   607.1'1764–dc23
                                        2014042430

Printed in the USA at Walsworth Publishing Company

CONTENTS

Texas State Technical College's 50th Anniversary Committee chose to implement a new tradition for TSTC graduates—the Stole of Gratitude. Pictured here, the stole is a gift from the TSTC chancellor to every 2015 graduate.

Preamble: Colonel James T. Connally

Texas State Technical College (TSTC), along with its individual campuses, has transitioned through a series of names in the fifty years since the 59th Texas Legislature passed legislation creating the state's first post-secondary school focused on vocational and technical training.

It was TSTC's first name, however, which gave the school its link to the storied and noble past of a decorated war hero. From 1965 to 1969, TSTC was known as the James Connally Technical Institute (JCTI), a name which tied "Connally Tech" to a former military base in Waco and to the friendship of two Texas Aggies working their way through college.

Colonel James Thomas Connally grew up in the Waco area. He was born in McGregor on June 12, 1910, and graduated from Waco High School in 1927. Following graduation from what was then called Texas A&M College in College Station, he joined the Army Air Corps in 1932.

While serving in the Philippines with the 19th Bombardment Group, Colonel Connally was awarded the Distinguished Flying Cross for a mission credited with destroying a Japanese tanker and rescuing twenty-three stranded American pilots. His career also earned him the Purple Heart, the Legion of Merit Cross, the Air Medal, a Presidential Citation, and the British Air Force Cross.

While serving as commander of the 504th Bombardment Group, Colonel Connally lost his life on May 29, 1945, when his plane exploded after being hit during a B-29 bombing mission over Yokohama, Japan.

On June 10, 1949, the Waco Army Air Field was renamed the Connally Air Force Base in honor of the Waco hero. By 1951, the base was known as the James Connally Air Force Base (JCAFB).

When it came time to name Texas's new technical school in Waco, it was Dr. Earl Rudder, president of Texas A&M University, who dictated the school's name (as stated in the *Waco Times-Herald* on April 5, 1965). "Jim Connally was an A. and M. graduate. We are proud of him down here at College Station. The James Connally Institute would be perfect," Rudder said. "Jim and I waited tables together at Sbisa Hall. I knew him well and will always admire him as a fine, brave, intelligent man."

JCAFB became home to the James Connally Technical Institute of Texas A&M University in 1965. Connally Tech was renamed Texas State Technical Institute (TSTI) in 1969 and separated from Texas A&M University. Finally, in 1991, the 72nd Legislature acknowledged TSTI's growth to multiple campuses and recognized the institute as a full college system with a new name, Texas State Technical College.

Colonel Connally's legacy, nevertheless, continues on the TSTC Waco campus with the Colonel James T. Connally Aerospace Center, which opened May 3, 2012—exactly seventy years after the May 1942 opening of the Waco Army Air Field. The 82,000-square-foot center houses aerospace operations for TSTC's airport, the largest in the nation owned and operated by a two-year public educational institution. In addition, the center offers high-tech aviation programs certified by the Federal Aviation Administration, including aviation maintenance, air traffic control, avionics, aircraft dispatch, and aircraft pilot training.

The four airfields, which eventually became campuses for Texas State Technical College, were economic engines within their communities. In the 1960s, all four were deactivated. The news left city leaders in host communities wondering if their communities would survive and looking for ways to fill the void.

(On loan to TSTC from Terry D. Cooper)

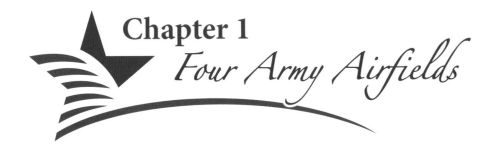

Chapter 1
Four Army Airfields

All four of Texas State Technical College's original campuses began as World War II army airfields with mission critical assignments in support of the US Army Air Forces. Waco Army Air Field trained pilots, while Harlingen Army Air Field served as a gunnery school. Amarillo Army Air Field trained aircrew, engine mechanics, and ground technicians.

As the sole training base for the Women Airforce Service Pilots (WASPs), however, it was Sweetwater's Avenger Field that laid claim to the most legendary mission of the four airfields. All but one class of the 1,074 women who earned their wings as WASPs graduated from Sweetwater. The women's intensive training program, which normally required nine months to complete, lasted 22.5 weeks and included everything taught to regular army pilots except gunnery and formation flying. Before being disbanded in 1944, the female pilots logged sixty million miles ferrying planes or cargo in most every type of American military aircraft.

Following WWII, all four of the airfields were deactivated.

By the time the United States became embroiled in the Korean conflict, the airfields were reactivated and transferred to the control of the US Air Force. Although the US Air Force adjusted specific assignments, each air base resumed a training and support mission. Generally, the air force bases were expanded and improved during this period. They varied in size from the James Connally Air Force Base's 2,100 acres in Waco to Avenger Field's 920 acres in Sweetwater. In addition to the runways and hangers associated with the airfields, most air bases were small, self-contained towns—complete with family housing, barracks, warehouses, medical and recreational facilities, libraries, office buildings, maintenance shops, and stores. Thousands of people lived and/or worked on them.

The air bases represented a huge part of the economy in each of the communities in which they were located. Through a series of realignments, all four of the air bases were, again, deactivated in the 1960s. In every case, the deactivation announcement left city leaders in host communities looking for ways to fill the void. Many of them became heroes, in their own right, as they fought to repurpose the soon-to-be-abandoned assets and acreage, which were once vibrant economic engines within their communities.

Harlingen Army Air Field

Waco Army Air Field

May 3, 1941
The War Department announces plans for an air-to-air and air-to-surface gunnery school to be located in Harlingen on donated land. Originally called the Harlingen Aerial Gunnery School or HAGS, the airfield's name was soon changed to the Harlingen Army Air Field when female army personnel objected to the acronym.

May 5, 1942
The Waco Army Air Field opens seven miles northeast of town as a pilot training school.

1941

The Air Base Years

April 1942
Located east of town on 1,532 acres, the Amarillo Army Air Field is activated as a technical training center for aircrew and ground mechanics.

May 14, 1942
The municipal airport in Sweetwater is leased for a dollar a year to the War Department for pilot training. It is soon renamed Avenger Field, the winning name in a local newspaper contest.

(Photos below and right courtesy of National WASP WWII Museum)

Colonel James T. Connally, official US Air Force photo, 3565th Navigation Training Squadron

February 21, 1943
Avenger Field becomes home to the Women Airforce Service Pilots (WASPs). By April, it is the only all-female air base and remains the only one in history.

1945
The Waco Army Air Field and Avenger Field are deactivated late in the year.

February 1946
The Harlingen Army Air Field is deactivated.

September 1946
The Amarillo Army Air Field is deactivated.

1948
Waco Army Air Field is reactivated for pilot training.

June 10, 1949
The Waco Army Air Field is renamed the Connally Air Force Base in memory of Colonel James T. Connally, a local pilot killed when his plane was hit by anti-aircraft fire over Japan.

June 1950
The United States, through a United Nations Security Council resolution, authorizes military intervention in Korea after North Korea invades South Korea.

March 1951
The Amarillo Army Air Field is reactivated as the Amarillo Air Force Base and becomes the first US Air Force training base devoted exclusively to jet mechanics.

March 1952
In response to pleas from city leaders and after Congress makes two appropriations, $15 million for reactivation and $12 million for rehabilitation, the US Air Force reactivates the airfield as the Harlingen Air Force Base for navigator training. Over thirteen thousand navigators will eventually train at the air base.

1950

1951
The Connally Air Force Base's name becomes James Connally Air Force Base, and all pilot training is discontinued. The base transitions to training navigators, radar operators, and bombardiers.

April 1, 1952
Avenger Field is reactivated as an auxiliary airfield for pilot training.

June 6, 1962
The Harlingen Air Force Base, now expanded to 1,400 acres, graduates its last class of navigators.

1963
The Harlingen Air Force Base, originally leased to the War Department by the City of Harlingen, converts to civilian use. Much of the land is eventually redeveloped into the Valley International Airport.

December 1964
The James Connally Air Force Base receives a deactivation notice.

August 1968
The US Air Force completes the final phase-out of personnel assigned to the James Connally Air Force Base.

December 11, 1968
Although deactivation was announced four years earlier, Amarillo Air Force Base graduates its last class of jet-engine mechanics. The base closes by the end of the year.

November 1969
After transitioning to an aircraft control and warning radar installation under the US Air Force Air Defense Command, Avenger Field closes as a military installation. The land and buildings convert back to the City of Sweetwater.

There is not a really high-level technical vocational training school in Texas or anywhere close to Texas… Earl, you ought to take over that air base at Waco and turn it into the most sophisticated technical vocational training institute in the country.

Governor John B. Connally
February 5, 1965

Chapter 2
A Governor's Vision

As the US Air Force made public the lists of air bases to be deactivated in the mid-1960s, community leaders in Waco, Harlingen, Amarillo, and Sweetwater were shocked as they anticipated the negative impact losing the air bases would have upon their communities.

The James Connally Air Force Base (JCAFB) in Waco, for example, comprised 2,100 acres and had an annual payroll of over $19 million with 4,034 assigned personnel and 835 civilian employees. Many felt Waco would never recover from the loss.

When appeals to keep the bases open failed, civic leaders in all four communities rallied to repurpose the installations. A Waco delegation made up of Harry Provence, Harlon Fentress, and John Henry "Jack" Kultgen was the first to find success.

Shortly after JCAFB's closure was announced, the delegation brought the base's plight to the attention of every policymaker they knew. Provence and Kultgen, in particular, were well connected with politicians in both Washington, DC, and Austin. They left detailed drawings and specifications of the facility with the governor's staff. Their hope was to repurpose JCAFB as an Air National Guard facility.

Governor John B. Connally visited JCAFB in December of 1964, but he had an entirely different vision for the facility. His concern was that Texas industry had no place to train workers. He felt JCAFB's existing facilities would be perfect for a training facility and its central location could benefit all of Texas. On February 5, 1965, the governor met in his office with President Earl Rudder of Texas A&M University and State Senator William Moore of Bryan. Governor Connally's purpose was to convince Rudder and the university to take ownership of the Waco air base in order to create "the most sophisticated technical vocational training institute in the country."

The very next day, Governor Connally met with the three men from Waco and told them that "the trouble with our program so far on higher education is that we're just asking for a little more of the same thing. Nobody has been bold enough to step out in a completely new field." Governor Connally wanted a new direction for higher education—one that focused on training workers to match industry needs—and he wanted it at the JCAFB.

In an emergency message on April 5, Governor Connally asked the 59th Legislature to grant Texas A&M University the authority to take over JCAFB and requested the initial appropriations to plan a new technical and vocational training school on its site. The enabling legislation, creating the James Connally Technical Institute of Texas A&M University, was signed into law on April 22, 1965—meaning the legislation was filed, passed by both chambers of the legislature, and was signed into law in under three weeks time.

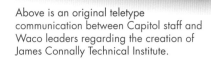

Above is an original teletype communication between Capitol staff and Waco leaders regarding the creation of James Connally Technical Institute.

T

CAPITOL STAFF THERE

JERRY: TAKE THE FOLLOWING MESSAGE TO BOB SALTER AND TELL HIM TO SHARE IT WITH MOORE AND THOMAS PLEASE:

THE FOLLOWING TELEGRAM WENT TODAY TO SPEAKER AND T TO HEATLY AS WELL AS TO GOVERNOR AND LIEUT GOV:

IF STATE PURCHASE OF JCAFB AT NEGOTIATION PRICE OF $5.25 MILLION IS DELAYED PAST DEADLINE OF OCT.4,) 1967, THE FOLLOWING MONETARY LOSSES TO THE STATE'S JAMES CONNALLY XXXXXDRXXXBASXXXXX TECHNICAL INSTITUTE WILL OCCUR: 300,000 HOUSING RENTALS; $50,000 2XXX WAREHOUSE RENTAL; $120,000 RENTAL OF OTHER FACILITIES FROM GENERAL DYNAMICS NOW ON BASE. IN ADDITION A MAJOR AIRLINE I IS NEGOTIATING FOR USE OF AIR STRIP IN NEAR FUTURE.
    MORE THAN THAT, BLEEDING PROCESS AS AIR FORCE PHASES OUT AT BASE WILL REMOVE MILLIONS OF DOLLARS IN PROPERTY WHICH ALREADY IS EARMARKED FOR CONNALLY TECH ON BASIS OF $5.25 MILLION PURCHASE AGREEMENT BEFORE OCT.4.
    THIS PURCHASE PRICE WAS NEGOTIATED AT REQUEST OF GOV. H JOHN CONNALLY IN ORDER TO SAVE STATE OF TEXA MXXX TEXAS MILLIONS OF DOLLARS IN FUTURE OPERATING COSTS AT CONNALLY TECH AND TO GIVE STATE FULL CONTROL OF FACL FACILITIES. THE GOVEN XXX GOVERNOR'S WORD TO THE HIGHES T OFFFICIALS OF NATIONAL GOVERNMENT IS AT STAKE IN THIS MATTER. THE ECONOMIC FUTURE OF TEXAS AS AN INDUSTRIAL STATE HINGES HEAVILY ON DEVELOPMENT OF CONNALLY TECH, A DEVELOPMENT WHICH CANNOT BE DONE UNLESS THIS PURCHASE IS ACCOMPLISHED PROMPTLY. (SU SIGNED BY FENTRESS KULTGEN AND PROVENCE).

JERRY: U THERE NOW?

YEP I 'M HERE ON DECK AND SW JUST WALKD WALKED IN. SALTER AS YOU KNOW, HAD LONG CONFERENCE WITH BARNES THIS AM AND THE WACO BOYS PRETTY GLUM ABOUT PROSPECTS AT THIS POINT.

WELL THE POINT OF THE TELEGRAMS TO THE FACE CARDS IS TO GET ON PAPER WHAT IS AT STAKE I N THIS, STARTING WITH DEADLINE ON PURCHASE...BARNES AND HEATLY APPARENTLY HAVENT UNDERSTOOD THAT THIS DEAL WAS WORKED OUT BETWEEN CONNALLY MCNAMARA AND WHITE HOUSE AND THE DEADLINE AINT SUBJECT TO JAZZING AROUND BY ANY UNDERLINGS OR BYSTANDERS.

THIS SW

I GOT A CALL FROM PRESTON WHILE AGO...HE GOT HIS COPY OF THE ABOVE TELEGRAM AND WANTED TO KNOW WHY WE WIRED HIM H WHEN HE HAS GOT HIS SIDE OF IT IN ORDER...I TOLD HIM WE WENT HIM SENT HIM A COPY FOR HIS INFO SO HE WOULD HAVE THE FIGURES... HE THINKS SENATE SIDE WILL RESCUE DEAL IN CONFERENCE IF IT COMES TO THAT.

OK WE WILL GO DELIVER THE TELEGRAM. HOUSE STILL WORKING ON APPROPRIATION BILL.

MIGHT SHOW EM MY FOOTNOTE ABOUT THE DEADLINE JUST TO BE SURE THEY QUIT LISTENING TO A COUPLE OF FED BUREAUCRATS FROM DALLAS WHO TRYING TO QUEER THINGS

OK
HA THANX

Texas A&M University President Earl Rudder

December 1964
The James Connally Air Force Base (JCAFB) receives a deactivation notice.

February 6, 1965
A delegation of Waco business leaders meet with the Texas governor, who shares his idea for a technical institute located at JCAFB.

April 13, 1965
The Texas Senate passes Senate Bill 487 by State Senator Murray Watson and State Senator William Moore, authorizing the creation of a state technical institute.

February 5, 1965
Governor John B. Connally meets with President Earl Rudder of Texas A&M University and State Senator William Moore of Bryan to discuss his desire to create a technical institute on the site of JCAFB in Waco and his intent that the institute be part of Texas A&M University.

April 5, 1965
Governor John B. Connally sends an emergency message to the 59th Legislature asking that Texas A&M University be given the authority to take control of JCAFB, valued at $57 million. Enabling legislation is introduced the same day.

April 15, 1965
Senate Bill 487 passes the Texas House of Representatives. Sponsors include the entire McLennan County delegation—State Representatives Jack Woods, Dick Cherry, and George Cowden, in addition to Representative David Haines from Bryan.

1964

The Creation of Connally Tech

An Opportunity for Women

After lunching with Governor John B. Connally on May 21, 1965, Dr. Earl Rudder and Dr. Roy Dugger flew to Houston to meet with the Texas A&M Board of Directors. A chief concern of the directors was whether the new institute would admit women. Dugger argued in their favor. "…I felt that we could…create a technical institute that would be a model for Texas and perhaps the nation, where women would have opportunity with men in terms of learning to earn a good living for themselves and their families."

Bright Future Lies Ahead for JCAFB and Waco

THE WACO TIMES-HERALD

DRIVE SAFELY · DRIVE CAREFULLY — SPEED SHOULD GO DOWN WITH THE SUN · CITY FINAL

SEVENTY-THIRD YEAR—NUMBER 77 · WACO, TEXAS. MONDAY EVENING, APRIL 5, 1965—20 PAGES · SINGLE COPY 10 CENTS

Governor Asks State Take JCAFB For Top Level Technical School

GOVERNOR JOHN B. CONNALLY
Propose New "Training Mission" for JCAFB

Base Offers Fine List Of Facilities

Six Major Training Areas

Waco C-C Pledges Full Cooperation

A&M Would Run Institute

Idea for Training Center Got Rolling Last December

WEATHER

GRADUATE OF A&M

James Connally Name Preferred

More Top News Inside

Ideal Location For Jr. College

PROPOSAL

TO ESTABLISH

JAMES CONNALLY TECHNICAL INSTITUTE

Texas A&M University
College Station, Texas

Bob Poage Announces First Institute Grant

1965

April 22, 1965
Governor John B. Connally signs legislation into law, creating Texas's first comprehensive vocational and technical training facility—the James Connally Technical Institute of Texas A&M University (JCTI).

May 21, 1965
Dr. Roy Dugger, national director of Manpower Development and Training at the US Department of Health, Education and Welfare, flies to Austin to meet with the Texas governor and President Earl Rudder of Texas A&M University in order to present a list of possible candidates to direct the new technical institute. Rudder asks Dugger to take the job.

June 25, 1965
Dr. Earl Rudder and members of the Texas A&M Board of Directors visit JCAFB to tour the facilities.

June 26, 1965
Dr. Roy Dugger is appointed vice president of Texas A&M University and director of JCTI.

July 30, 1965
JCTI receives its first federal grant for $25,000 to develop a Manpower Technical Skill Center.

August 3, 1965
Colonel Jasper Bell, commander of JCAFB, presents the first building to Texas A&M University for JTCI. Dr. Roy Dugger, along with his family, arrives within two days and immediately sets up an administrative office.

September 2, 1965
Frank J. Konecny, one of the three men Dr. Roy Dugger recommended for his job, is the first to join JCTI as staff. Konecny became the first dean of JCTI.

AMERICAN SOCIETY
FOR QUALITY CONTROL
WACO SECTION

INVITES YOU TO ATTEND

The 1966 Spring
QUALITY CONTROL
TRAINING PROGRAM

*Fundamentals
Of
Dimensional
Metrology*

TO BE HELD AT

JAMES CONNALLY TECHNICAL
INSTITUTE
WACO, TEXAS

FUNDAMENTALS OF
DIMENSIONAL METROLOGY

WHY? WHEN? WHERE?

The advance of civilization is demonstrably related to man's ability to measure. This is even truer today than in antiquity. Measurement is truly a universal language. Where every other communication must be translated, all industrial people today recognize the same standards of length, and convert in and out of each other's systems of measurement.

As never before, the ability of an engineer, a chemist, a biologist, or a physicist to test his ideas hinges upon his understanding of measurement.

Now, at the threshold of the space age, "good enough" has been pushed beyond the borders of belief. Yesterday's standards and instruments can fulfill only their new functions through the imagination and ingenuity of the new breed of industrial specialists, the Quality Control people. Working with statistics and electronic computers, they regulate every phase of modern life which requires mass-produced products.

However, no matter how fast their computers can multiply ten-digit figures or how specifically their calculations can predict production, everything the Quality Control people do depends upon the informa-

These are the new aristocrats. Their responsible employment is needed at every level from production inspection to comparing master standards to the wave length of light. Those who specialize in measurement lead adventurous lives. They are present at both the births and deaths of new products, new scientific achievements, and new campaigns. Few decisions are made without their valued counsel.

It is the purpose of this course to prepare the student with a thorough understanding of the methods by which accurate data is assembled for analysis prior to acceptance of a product.

The standard measuring instruments will be discussed in the order in which you probably will encounter them, from the least precise to the most precise. Far more important, some rules will be developed to guide you in the selection of the best instrument for any given dimensional measurement.

The course will be presented by a qualified instructor at the James Connally Technical Institute, Waco, Texas beginning 11 January 1966. Classroom sessions will be two hours each, meeting one night each week for ten weeks.

An excellent text book, "Fundamentals of Dimensional Metrology", will be furnished the student which he will retain upon completion of the course. A

No. 113

WACO, TEXAS, 2 February 1966

PAY TO THE
ORDER OF *James Connally Technical Institute* $448.00

Four Hundred Forty Eight 00/100 DOLLARS

Community STATE BANK
WACO, TEXAS

WACO SECTION
AMERICAN SOCIETY FOR QUALITY CONTROL
By *B. W. Price* President
E. L. Brickhouse Treasurer

This check was the first money received by James Connally Technical Institute. It was for payment of costs associated with the first course taught at Connally Tech—Fundamentals of Dimensional Metrology—which was sponsored by the Waco Section-American Society for Quality Control.

Waco Tribune-Herald
WACO NEWS-TRIBUNE— *Voice of the Central Texas Empire*—THE WACO TIMES-HERALD

WACO, TEXAS, SATURDAY MORNING, SEPT. 10, 1966 —24 PAGES

Don't Plan Too Small, Tech Told

Money No Problem Budget Board Says

By ROGER CANTRELL
Waco Times-Herald Staff

House of Representative members of the Legislative Budget Board cheered the administration of James Connally Technical Institute Friday afternoon by giving their assurance that the school has no reason to worry about money.

"You have the support of the state legislature," House Speaker Ben Barnes told Dr. Roy Dugger at the end of a short, delayed rain-wet inspection tour of Connally Tech.

Dugger, president of the institute, told the legislators that Connally Tech is at least $225,000 short of what it needs to operate until next Sept. 1. He suggested an emergency appropriation from the legislature as the solution to the problem.

His plea was directed to Barnes; Rep. W. S. Heatly of Paducah, chairman of the House Appropriations Committee; and members Rep. Maurice Pipkin of Brownsville; Rep. Ben Atwell of Dallas; and Rep. Gus Mutscher of Brenham.

The assurance came mainly from Barnes and Heatly.

HOUSE OF REPRESENTATIVES Speaker Ben Barnes, right, is greeted on his arrival in Waco Friday by Dr. Roy Dugger, left, president of James Connally Technical Institute, and Texas A&M President Earl Rudder. Barnes was one of five state representatives who toured Connally Tech and Waco State Home. (John Bennett photo)

January 11, 1966
The first class, a continuing education course in the fundamentals of dimensional metrology, begins at JCTI with seventy students.

January 21, 1966
US Congressman William R. Poage from Waco announces a $361,922 federal grant award to JCTI for instructors and training in three occupational areas under the Manpower Development Training Act of 1965. Areas include general maintenance mechanics, refrigeration mechanics, and water sewage technology.

April 5, 1966
The first full-time classes open at JCTI with fifty-eight students.

August 1966
JCTI receives approval for three additional training programs in welding, drafting, and farm equipment mechanics under the Manpower Development Training Act.

September 1966
Approximately 230 students enroll in JCTI's first two-year programs. Courses include building materials technology and marketing; chemical technology; civil and highway technology; construction technology; dental laboratory technology; electronic technology; equipment mechanics; industrial design, drafting, and illustration technology; and welding technology.

December 10, 1966
US Congressman William R. Poage visits JCTI for the first time.

Dr. Roy W. Dugger: "We're Talking About You."

When Dr. Roy Wesley Dugger stepped off the plane in Austin on May 21, 1965, to have lunch with Governor John B. Connally and Dr. Earl Rudder, president of Texas A&M University, he carried the resumes of men he felt were qualified to head the state's new vocational and technical training institute.

Dugger knew the institute was a special project for Governor Connally, one he had pushed through the legislature only a month earlier. He also knew the governor had tasked Rudder with making the project a reality on the James Connally Air Force Base in Waco.

Rudder had asked Dugger to bring the resumes to Austin, but the trip was more than a favor for an old friend and fellow Aggie. Dugger wanted the governor's technical institute to succeed. He well understood the country's need for trained technicians. After stints in the US Navy during World War II and Korea, Dugger had spent his entire career in technical education in Texas, Oklahoma, and now Washington, D.C.

"I always had in mind, from high school years forward, to be a vocational agriculture teacher," Dugger said in a 1982 interview. For many years, his parents were tenant farmers and eventually bought a farm in Collin County, Texas. His early experiences on the farm sealed Dugger's interest in training adults, particularly adult farmers, how to make a better living for themselves and their families through mechanized farming techniques and irrigation farming.

Dugger was an electronics technician in the navy and became an electronics instructor in charge of curriculum development for navy personnel. He was also part of the first team that electronically measured the distance from the earth to the moon. He understood the changes technology was bringing to agriculture and to the workforce. He believed the civilian workforce of the 1960s and 1970s needed to have an opportunity to enter into the highly technical fields. A specialized vocational and technical training center may have been Governor Connally's vision for Texas, but it was Dugger's passion.

Dugger had parlayed his interest in technical training into federal appointments under two presidents. He had played touch football on the White House lawn with the Kennedy entourage and was one of the first called to brief Lyndon B. Johnson upon his return to Washington, DC, after the Dallas tragedy

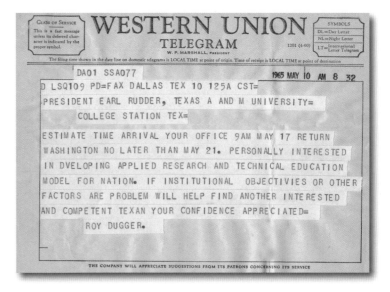

WITHIN FEW DAYS

Dugger Will Assume Duties at Air Base

in 1963. At the time of his Austin lunch with the governor and Rudder, Dugger was considered a career bureaucrat with a GS-16 ranking, a senior executive on the federal government's pay scale. As both the national director of Manpower Development and Training and the deputy assistant commissioner for vocational-technical education in the US Office of Education, he had every intention of delivering the contents of his briefcase and returning to Washington.

Rudder refused to consider anyone who was not a Texas Aggie, which narrowed Dugger's list of candidates to three names. Following lunch in Austin, Rudder borrowed the governor's plane and asked Dugger to fly with him to Houston to meet with the Texas A&M University Board of Directors, who were holding a special meeting in the Tenneco Building to consider a $300,000 bond issuance.

Once the two men boarded the plane, Rudder surprised his guest by dismissing the rest of the resumes in Dugger's briefcase. "Now, Roy, we want you to get off these recommendations. We're talking about you." With those words, he offered Dugger a position as vice president of Texas A&M University and director of the James Connally Technical Institute (JCTI) at a salary in keeping with that of a senior federal executive. In fact, it was a salary higher than that of the president of the university.

Dr. and Mrs. Roy Dugger are welcomed to the James Connally Air Force Base.

With a handshake contingent upon his family's approval, Dugger accepted. The Texas A&M Board of Directors formally approved Dugger's hiring and salary at a regular meeting of the board on June 26.

Shortly after Dugger moved his family to Texas to accept the position at JCTI, he returned to Washington, DC, to receive the Distinguished Service Award for Civilian Service in a ceremony on the White House lawn. Dugger made many trips to Washington during the early days of JCTI to finalize the transfer of the air base's assets to the state and to secure grant funding for JCTI. His Washington connections proved invaluable and, in many cases, made the difference between success and failure for the fledgling institute.

Rapid Progress

During his first visit to James Connally Technical Institute on December 10, 1966, Congressman William R. Poage stated, "They've made tremendous progress in the short time they've had. I don't see how they've moved as fast as they did."

Poage, whose district included Waco, was a member of the US House of Representatives from 1936 to 1978. He played a key role in the campus's transition from US Air Force control to state control and was instrumental in many of the initial grants which funded JCTI programs.

In 1967, the first graduating class of full-time students in a twelve-month program at James Connally Technical Institute asked the wife of the Texas lieutenant governor to select the school's official flower. Mrs. Preston Smith selected the Yellow Rose of Texas.

Connally Tech Paying Off As Texas Industrial Lure

(Courtesy of General Dynamics)

Lieutenant Governor Preston Smith greets Connally Tech students on the eve of the first graduation ceremony for full-time students.

The State of Texas
Office of the Lieutenant Governor
Austin

PRESTON SMITH
LIEUTENANT GOVERNOR
PRESIDENT OF THE SENATE

March 23, 1967

Mr. Frank J. Konecny
James Connally Technical Institute
Waco, Texas

Dear Frank:

Just a note to personally express my deep appreciation for the wonderful hospitality accorded me recently while I was in Waco to attend and participate in the first graduation exercises of the James Connally Technical Institute.

I thoroughly enjoyed every minute of my trip there and especially the fact that I was made the very first graduate of this new institute.

Sincerely,

Preston Smith

PS:afp

1967

February 11, 1967
JCTI holds groundbreaking ceremonies to widen the airport's runaway as part of an agreement with General Dynamics Corporation authorizing the use of an airport hangar to modify B-58 Bombers. Keynote speakers include US Congressman William R. Poage and State Senator Murray Watson.

February 26, 1967
Texas A&M University Board of Directors grants JCTI authority to award associate's degrees in applied science to graduates in two-year programs.

March 16, 1967
JCTI conducts its first graduation ceremony for full-time students in a twelve-month program financed by the Manpower Development Training Act. Lieutenant Governor Preston Smith serves as commencement speaker and, at the students' request, receives the first honorary certificate of graduation from JCTI.

April 7, 1967
State Representative William S. Heatly, chairman of the House Appropriations Committee, speaks at the graduation ceremony for twenty-nine arc welders. He announces Governor John B. Connally's intention to ask the 60th Legislature for $5.25 million to purchase JCAFB for permanent use as a technical institute.

July 10, 1967
US Congressman William R. Poage announces approval of a $1.935 million US Air Force contract with General Dynamics Corporation. Minutes later, the first B-58 Bombers arrive in Waco. JCTI's training partnership with General Dynamics is credited with bringing the industrial giant to Waco.

Governor John B. Connally visits Connally Tech in October 1967.

Is It a Base... Or, Is It a Campus?

Although the Texas Legislature moved quickly after the federal government issued the December 1964 deactivation notice for the James Connally Air Force Base (JCAFB), military personnel did not actually vacate the facility until September of 1968.

Nevertheless, "Connally Tech" established administrative offices on the base in August of 1965 and began teaching classes by the following January. The intervening three-plus years between school start-up and air base phase-out proved to be a unique and sometimes humorous dance between school administrators and military personnel.

At the time, the typical process for deactivating a military installation was to strip the facility of all removable assets and to deed the land and buildings to a local governmental entity to be repurposed. There were intrinsic problems with the federal government's "give-away" program, however. In a 1982 interview, Dr. Roy Dugger, James Connally Technical Institute's (JCTI) first director, said the give-away program was not the way to acquire federal property and make it useful for civilian purposes. "There're several things wrong with a gift; it takes 20 to 30 years to acquire it. During that time, nobody owns it, neither the federal government nor the state. The buildings deteriorate." Dugger knew the legislature would never finance new instructional facilities for JCTI if the state did not have clear title to the property.

As a result, he and Dr. Earl Rudder, president of Texas A&M University, proposed the state buy the facility from the federal government, an idea which took considerable negotiation at the legislature. Dugger wanted land, buildings, furnishings, and equipment—everything "except the whine of the jet airplanes." Because it took two years to settle on a purchase price and to secure the needed legislative appropriations, JCTI became tenants of the US Air Force and began operations before the facility belonged to the state.

JCAFB was eventually appraised at over $57 million, but the federal government accepted a purchase price of $5.25 million. Governor John B. Connally presented a check for the full amount to federal officials in a formal ceremony on October 14, 1967, with over three thousand people present. With that, the US Air Force became tenants of JCTI and Texas A&M University.

US President Lyndon B. Johnson and Governor Connally, a former Secretary of the Navy, were instrumental in keeping the air force on site for as long as possible. The thought was to give the state time to assume full financial responsibility for the 2,100-acre air base, which included 866 houses, two hundred other buildings, and a large airport. The state's original appropriation to open JCTI was a mere $200,000, a sum which would not even pay the annual electric bill at JCAFB. According to Dugger, "It cost $1 million for one year to just open the gates and that was without doing anything within the facility."

The challenge for Dugger was to grow an educational institution unlike anything ever attempted in Texas while maneuvering around military personnel, and he had to do it on a miniscule state budget supplemented by federal grants. To help manage the military, Dugger hired Major General Robert M. Stillman (Retired) as the assistant director of JCTI.

Stillman was a decorated bomber pilot during World War II and the retiring commander of the Sheppard Technical Training Center at Sheppard Air Force Base in Wichita Falls. According to Dugger, Stillman's job was "to see that every building was turned over to Texas A&M University in good condition with all the desks, chairs, machine tools, hand tools, hammers, squares, and everything else in tact in that building." The job proved to be a test of wills as the air force, and every other military installation within driving distance, was accustomed to stripping a base clean once a deactivation notice was made public.

The stories were repetitious. Empty eighteen-wheeler trucks would arrive on site, and Stillman would end up stopping airmen mid-load until calls were made to Washington, DC. Then, the same trucks would be unloaded. Army crews from Fort Hood would be caught dismantling equipment, and Stillman or Dugger would tell them to grab a soft drink in the snack bar. Calls would be made, new orders would be issued, and the same crews would reassemble the equipment in order to return everything to working order. Dugger later summarized the experience by saying, "…we had a lot of fun that way."

The property issue was finally resolved one morning after a three-hour negotiation about assets with a senior civilian aide to a three-star US Air Force general. Frustrated with the negotiation's progress, Dugger walked across the room and picked up the telephone. "I looked at my watch and knew that my friend in the White House would be there about that time… It was the only time he [the civilian aide to the general] ever talked to his boss, the commander-in-chief of the Armed Forces in the United States."

The friend was President Johnson. Negotiations over; problem solved.

Texas Governor John B. Connally presents a check for $5.25 million to US General Services Administration Administrator Lawson Knott Jr. for the purchase of the James Connally Air Force Base.

Late July 1967
In partnership with Springfield Technical Institute of Massachusetts, JCTI receives $335,000 to begin the nation's first training in biomedical equipment technology.

September 1967
JCTI begins its second full year of operation with sixty-two faculty members, over one thousand students, and thirty-three courses of study.

October 14, 1967
Over three thousand people attend dedication ceremonies for JCTI. Governor John B. Connally presents the US Air Force a check for $5.25 million to purchase all of JCAFB.

1967

August 10, 1967
JCTI graduates twenty-eight students from the first one-year class under state-funded programs, a heavy construction equipment mechanics course.

September 1967
Dr. Roy Dugger, JCTI director, announces plans for a bilingual training center to be located in Harlingen, as well as plans for a third JCTI campus to be located in Amarillo.

Entertainer Sonny Bono traveled as part of US Vice President Hubert Humphrey's entourage.

THE TECH TIMES

VOLUME 3, NO. 2   JAMES CONNALLY TECHNICAL INSTITUTE   NOVEMBER 11, 1968

WACO BE mine IN '69 HHH TEXAS

The Tech Times

VOLUME 3, NO. 3   JAMES CONNALLY TECHNICAL INSTITUTE   DECEMBER 17, 1968

JCTI Now 'Fully Accredited'

Revolving Tenants

From June of 1965, following the legislature's decision to create a technical institute on the James Connally Air Force Base, until all military operations ceased in September of 1968, the 2,100 acres which comprised the base's territory served as both a military base and an educational campus. Initially, the technical institute was a tenant of the US Air Force. By October of 1967, the air force transitioned into being tenants of Connally Tech. While constructing a permanent location in Waco, McLennan Community College was also a tenant—of both—first, the air force; then, Connally Tech. As might be expected, military personnel refused to call the facility anything but a "base," and educators refused to call it anything but a "campus."

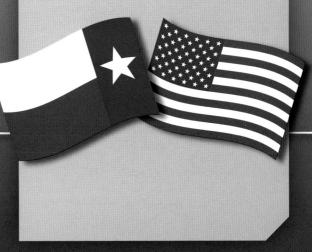

October 1, 1968
The Federal Aviation Administration grants JCTI authorization to operate a civil airport.

October 22, 1968
US Vice President Hubert Humphrey and US Congressman William R. Poage visit JCTI. The congressman announces $1 million in funding for an Automotive Manpower Center to be named for John Henry "Jack" Kultgen, then chairman of the Texas Highway Commission and a Waco civic leader.

August 2, 1968
JCTI awards its first associate's degrees to 153 students. All graduates are employed before graduation ceremonies occur.

December 6, 1968
JCTI receives accreditation from the Southern Association of Colleges and Schools.

The Committee is of the opinion that James Connally Technical Institute should not remain under the jurisdiction of Texas A&M University or any other system but should be operated as a separate entity. We recommend that the Legislature consider the creation, or re-creation, of the James Connally Technical Institute as a separate institutional system, with an independent governing board, and with a clearly defined role and scope.

House Education Committee Report
"Vocational and Technical Education
State of Texas / 1968"
*First interim study to be made by a full
standing committee in either chamber of
the Texas Legislature*

Chapter 3
The Making of a Technical Institute

When President Earl Rudder first took Dr. Roy Dugger, a Washington bureaucrat, to meet with the Texas A&M University Board of Directors in May of 1965, not everyone on the board fully understood what Governor John B. Connally intended for the James Connally Air Force Base (JCAFB).

Some were not even familiar with technical education or what an appropriate curriculum would entail, but the board felt it should cooperate with the governor.

The board was not alone. According to Betty June Barkley, James Connally Technical Institute's (JCTI) second employee and Dugger's secretary, "We had such a task of educating the public about what technical education actually was. They considered us more or less a job corps-type school, and they seemed to think that it was only for students who had very low IQs and could not make it in the so-called college or university system."

Even those instrumental in bringing the school to Waco had doubts. Harry Provence, the long-time editor of the *Waco News-Tribune* and the *Waco Times-Herald,* was one of several community leaders who made finding a new use for JCAFB a priority. He counted both Governor Connally and US President

Lyndon B. Johnson as personal friends and authored *Lyndon B. Johnson: A Biography* for Fleet Publishing Corporation in 1964. In his first-person account as part of the Waco History Project, Provence described his bewildered reaction when told of the governor's plan, "What is a technical institute?"

By the time Provence was asked to speak at the August 1968 commencement, however, he understood. Calling the graduation a breakthrough, he said of JCTI that "nothing of its kind had ever been attempted in this state." The graduation was the first at JCTI to award two-year degrees. All 153 graduates had jobs before they walked across the stage to receive their diplomas— most receiving as many as six job offers.

The graduation ceremonies Provence witnessed almost never happened, though, because of the Texas Legislature's own confusion about the structure of a technical institute. The 1965 legislation creating JCTI prohibited the institute from awarding associate's degrees, something that was not granted until February of 1967. A handwritten floor amendment in the Texas House of Representatives required JCTI's programs to be approved by both the State Board of Vocational Education, which was under what is now the Texas Education Agency, and by the precursor to the Texas Higher Education Coordinating Board. In other words, JCTI was to be governed by two separate state agencies, in addition to the Texas A&M University Board of Directors.

JCTI's role continued to be a source of confusion in the 1969 debate over the legislation which severed the institute from Texas A&M University. When the 61st Texas Legislature first considered House Bill 137, the new name for JCTI was to be the Manpower Resources System. A committee amendment changed the name to State Technical Institute of Texas. A floor amendment changed the name a final time to Texas State Technical Institute (TSTI). Legislators still remained unclear about which state agency should govern the institute's programs. Although there were multiple amendments on the matter, final bill language continued to require program approval from both the State Board of Technical Education and the Coordinating Board, Texas College and University System.

The confusion also led to three Senate filibusters against the legislation. In the end, House Bill 137 survived the filibusters and even survived a last-minute recall by State Senator Murray Watson to insert language granting revenue bond authority to a newly created board of regents. Governor Preston Smith signed House Bill 137, as amended and recalled, on May 9, 1969. In addition to changing JCTI's name and severing the school from Texas A&M University, the legislation created TSTI as a stand-alone institution and authorized additional campuses in Cameron and Potter Counties, which became TSTI's Rio Grande Campus in Harlingen and TSTI's Mid-Continent Campus in Amarillo.

Although confusion abounded about the name and the role of the state's first technical school, Dugger was the one person who always understood the vision. In fact, even as he left that first meeting with the Texas A&M University Board of Directors in May 1965, he felt he would have the freedom to establish something unique to Texas and a model for the nation.

Reflecting that Dugger was the right person to oversee the school's foundation, Barkley said of her old boss, "...he had great visions and dreams." Eventually, Dugger was able to bring clarity to his vision and show Texas exactly what a technical institute could be.

As stated previously in this report, James Connally Technical Institute in Waco has developed several badly needed skilled and semi-skilled training programs and the rapid and efficient organization at that school has been phenomenal. It is our hope...that this institution will be developed into a truly first rate vocational-technical institute.

House Education Committee Report
"Vocational and Technical Education
State of Texas/1968"

> Section 1. The name of James Connally Technical Institute of Texas A&M University is changed to the Manpower Resources System.

The name originally considered for Texas State Technical Institute as evidenced by this excerpt from House Bill 137 from the 61st Legislature.

THE TECH TIMES
JAMES CONNALLY TECHNICAL INSTITUTE
APRIL 15, 1969

Separation Vote Put Off--And Off

★ ★ ★   ★ ★ ★

Observations In Austin

As Smoke Clears, Bill Still Alive

By McDONALD WILLIAMS

The spirit of Sam Houston still lingers in the Texas Senate when it comes to passing bills out of committee. However, today's battles consist of loaded questions and answers instead of loaded fists and guns.

On March 24, a very exciting day was spent by this reporter at the Texas State Capitol. Not having been in the Senate chambers for many years, I had forgotten how fiery the pros and cons can get when it comes to passing a bill out of committee to the Senate floor where it can be voted on.

The bill in question was H.B. 137. Previously passed and approved by the House of Representatives, it had to be passed by the Senate Committee as Senate Bill 115, and there was quite a lot of opposition to the bill.

H.B. 137 separates James Connally Technical Institute from the Texas A & M system, and would establish a board of regents for JCTI. This would give Connally Tech the power to govern itself and maintain separate campuses at Harlingen and Amarillo.

After an afternoon of waiting and listening to witnesses for and against a bill (which didn't pass) that would give the State Board of Dental Examiners broader powers, the senators were surely beginning to tire

of testimonials that ranged from how people had their false teeth made in 1928 to the merits of mouthwash and the effects of tooth powder on dentures.

After a couple of short and quick passages of other bills, the Senate finally got down to business on H. B. 137 and the fireworks started (thank goodness senators no longer wear sidearms) which kept me on the edge of my seat.

The chief opponent of H.B. 137 didn't want to kill the bill entirely, but wanted to amend it so

(See Observations, page 4)

The score was 8-to-8 just before the end of this hearing—a Senate committee session crucial to the fate of the Connally Tech separation bill. It took the chairman's final vote (making the score 9-to-8) before the bill survived and was sent on to the Senate floor. This photo shows some of the people who were in on the action: Standing, two proponents of the bill, Sen. James Bates of Edinburgh (left) and Dr. Roy Dugger, director of JCTI; also (in the foreground, in front of Bates) Sen. Jack Strong of Longview, the main force against the bill.

House Education Committee Report
Vocational and Technical Education
State of Texas / 1968

The Committee is of the opinion that James Connally Technical Institute should not remain under the jurisdiction of Texas A & M University or any other system but should be operated as a separate entity. We recommend that the Legislature consider the creation, or re-creation, of the James Connally Technical Institute as a separate institutional system, with an independent governing board, and with a clearly defined role and scope.

As stated previously in this report, James Connally Technical Institute in Waco has developed several badly needed skilled and semi-skilled training programs and the rapid and efficient organization at that school has been phenomenal. It is our hope, however, that this institution will be developed into a truly first rate vocational-technical institute.

March 1968
The Education Committee in the Texas House of Representatives issues a report confirming the need for a "first class" training institute and recommending James Connally Technical Institute (JCTI) be separated from Texas A&M University and be given an independent governing board.

February 4, 1969
State Representative Bob Salter and State Senator Murray Watson introduce legislation in the 61st Legislature to make JCTI an independent institution.

1968

September 1968
Enrollment on the Waco campus reaches 1,348 students. The US Air Force completes the phase out of all military operations at Connally Tech.

April 24, 1969
After surviving three filibusters, House Bill 137 passes the Texas Senate.

JCTI Stands on Its Own

THE TECH TIMES

Vol. 3. No 6   May, 1969

Divorce Now Final; A&M Ties Are Cut

Separation... It's Just The Beginning

Friday, May 9, a day that went by without fanfare at Connally Tech was probably the most important day in the history of the Institute. The same quiet atmosphere did not prevail in Austin, however, as Governor Preston Smith signed the bill into law which so many people have worked long and hard to see passed. With its signing, James Connally Tech became not only an independent institute, but the corner stone in a whole new system of vocational technical schools.

The change certainly did not seem too dramatic to most students. Surely none awoke the next moring feeling as if a revolution had occured. The change is, however, real and vital. It is the freedom of JCTI to create its own image and expand freely to meet the growing needs of Texas and the Southwest. It means that Connally Tech will not have to tag at the coattails of A&M for funds or permission to expand programs to meet increasing demands.

The bill that changed the name of Connally Tech to the Texas State Technical Institute will be going into effect on September 1. It represents the end of a three month struggle to pass the measure. Supporters were constantly harrassed by filibusters in the Senate, the most staunch opposition coming from Senator Strong of Longview.

The constant opposition to the bill was mostly due to the fear of the junior colleges that Connally Tech would be the recipient of state funds that would otherwise go to them. Amendments to appease the junior colleges were passed. They prohibit the duplication of the courses offered by the junior colleges near-by. It also makes all programs of the Institute subject to the approval of the State Board of Vocational Colleges to prevent such overlapping.

Sites have been selected for the two satellite campuses at Harlingen and Amarillo. Connally Tech is presently operating a campus at Harlingen, but the property does not yet belong to JCTI. Its deed is held by the Harlingen Area Council of Governments, but Connally Tech expects to purchase the property soon. The property which has been selected for the Amarillo campus carries a price tag of approximately $6 million. Officials of JCTI hope to bring the price

PRESTON SMITH
GOVERNOR OF TEXAS

Photo by Justus White

Administrative officials and members of the Student Congress of Connally Tech were witnesses to the signing of the bill that officially separated JCTI from Texas A&M University. Pictured here are l to r: James Alexander, Aldon Bade, Governor Preston Smith, Senator Dave Allred, and Dr. Roy W. Dugger.

down to about $2.5 million before the purchase is made. Both of these sites are, like the Waco campus, deactivated Air Force bases.

This brings the supporters of JCTI to grips with another piece of legislation that is necessary to the success of the system. In order for the Institute to buy property for its campuses, money must be raised through the sale of revenue bonds. Such bonds must be authorized through the Texas legislature. Senator Watson attempted to add the necessary bond sale authorization to the separation bill itself by means of a resolution, but it never came to a vote in the house.

'Leave Your Guns At Home, Son'

At the beginning of this trimester, the administration of JCTI re-asserted the school's position on the possession of firearms on the campus. The only individuals allowed to carry firearms in their automobiles or on their persons are the duly appointed police officers.

Students are, however, allowed to retain guns if they are brought to the office of campus security and left for safe keeping. Firearms are to be dis-assembled when they are checked in, and are to remain so while being carried in the car and from a hunting trip. The office of campus security has defined "dis-assembled" as when the gun is incapable of being discharged accidentally or otherwise, such as having the bolt or firing pin removed.

Council Will Wake You Up

Tickets are on sale for an Arvin AM-FM clock radio with a snooze alarm automatic cut-off timer. The radio is valued at $50.

The drawing is being sponsored by the student council, and all proceeds will be entered into the council treasury. Contributions will be 50¢ each, and can be gotten from any student congress member.

Observations In Austin
Governor Gives OK, Bill Now Final
By McDonald Williams

Governor Preston Smith, on May 9, signed the bill separating James Connally Technical Institute from Texas A&M University, and with a handshake from Dr. Roy Dugger, director of the Institute, it became official.

With the signing of this bill, JCTI will become Texas State Technical Institute on September 1, with a board of nine regents to operate the entire system with its main campus at Waco, and also campuses at Harlingen and Amarillo.

To some it may not seem so important, but it means that now technical educators can begin to lift Texas out of the dark ages of technical education and give citizens the opportunity to obtain the education and know-how needed to succeed in today's highly technical and scientific world.

It would seem the struggle is over but like the old saying, a battle has been won but the war still continues. The sponsors of this bill, Senator Murray Watson and Representatives Bob Thomas and Bob Salter must now draft a separate bill to allow the Board of Regents to finance programs. This will take separate legislation.

On this memorable occasion there was a large crowd in attendance. Approximately 50 people were present from JCTI, including Dean Morris Webb, Dean of Students Bob Gaines and the officers of the Student Congress.

Many business and civic leaders from Waco were on hand to witness the signing, plus a delegation from the Harlingen campus accompanied by prominent supporters of our school from the valley area including Senator James Bates, of Edinburg a staunch ally and fighter for technical education.

Our news party was headed by director of public relations,

(Continued on Page 4)

Texas State Technical Institute logo

1969

May 6, 1969
State Senator Murray Watson recalls the JCTI legislation in order to insert new language granting the institute's board the authority to issue revenue bonds.

May 9, 1969
Governor Preston Smith signs House Bill 137 into law.

August 1969
JCTI graduates its last class of two hundred students in one- and two-year programs under Texas A&M University.

September 1, 1969
Ceremonies on JCTI mark the transfer of the school from Texas A&M University. With the legislation and the transfer, JCTI becomes Texas State Technical Institute (TSTI).

September 10, 1969
Governor Preston Smith appoints the first members of the TSTI Board of Regents.

Regents of TSTI Hold Organizational Session

The first Board of Regents of the Texas State Technical Institute met for three hours Monday, partly in closed session, working out details of an $8,081,576 budget, appointing school officials, and adopting organizational resolutions.

The nine member board, meeting on the Connally campus, elected J. H. Kultgen, prominent Waco businessman, chairman of the board and appointed Dr. Roy Dugger president. John W. Nigliazzo of Hearne was elected vice chairman and Henry C. Schulte of Mexia was named third executive committee member.

Following his election Kultgen said that Texas is beginning to feel the effect of trained personnel on the economy and pledged his support to the betterment of the Institute.

Five vice presidents were named to serve under Dr. Dugger in governing the three-campus educational complex. Morris Webb, former Connally Tech dean, was named senior vice president. His TSTI duties will include fiscal affairs, administrative policy, and liaison with senior management and labor executives throughout Texas.

Dr. Jack E. Tompkins, former associate dean for research and development, was appointed vice president in charge of the Connally campus. Milton Schiller was named vice president of the Rio Grande campus in Harlingen and vice president for development.

Lt. Col. (ret.) Hill W. Bensley will wear two caps under new TSTI organization: vice president in charge of the proposed Mid Continent campus at Amarillo and secretary to the Board of Regents.

In other appointments, the board named Allen Weed former law partner of Sen. Murray Watson as board legal counsel and Theodore Talbot formerly associated with Paul Quinn College, as assistant to the president. The office of comptroller was left vacant.

During a closed executive procedure, the board hashed out details of a $8,081,576 budget. The budget shows an estimated tuition income of $213,796 and funds from other sources at $1,042,300. State general appropriations will then be in excess of $6,800,000. This meeting was the regents' first opportunity to look at the budget.

The board also awarded interim authority to the institute president to hire or fire any person employed by TSTI with the exception of certain general officials. Their appointments require confirmation of the board.

In basic organizational procedure, the board approved three resolutions as recommended by the president. In the first of these, the First

See TSTI REGENTS, Page 2

First Board of Regents of the Texas State Technical Institute
September, 1969

 Jack H. Kultgen
 John Nigliazzo
 Yancey Price
 Joe Garza
 Russell Watson
 Henry Schulte
 Richard Thomas
F. V. Wallace
 Harold Tate

September 21, 1969
The TSTI Board of Regents holds its first meeting and elects John Henry "Jack" Kultgen chairman of the board. Dr. Roy Dugger becomes president of the TSTI complex and names five vice presidents.

October 24, 1969
Walter F. Albritton is the first to receive a pilot's license at TSTI.

November 22, 1969
US Congressman William R. Poage visits TSTI to review plans for the J. H. Kultgen Automotive Center.

December 19, 1969
TSTI presents its first honorary degree to State Senator Murray Watson at the mid-year graduation ceremony. Over sixty students receive certificates or diplomas.

I have been with Texas State Technical College since the idea came along. For me, it has been like birthing a child. I have seen him crawl; I have seen him walk; and I now see him run. TSTC is very special to me.

State Senator Murray Watson Jr.
Texas House of Representatives, 1957–1963
Texas Senate, 1963–1973

Former State Senator Murray Watson Jr.

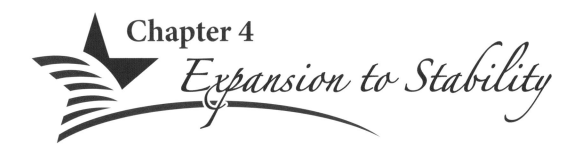

Chapter 4
Expansion to Stability

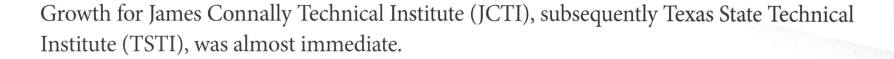

Growth for James Connally Technical Institute (JCTI), subsequently Texas State Technical Institute (TSTI), was almost immediate.

Military bases all over Texas had received deactivation notices in the mid-to-late 1960s, and communities were actively looking for something to fill the void. Waco had been successful with JCTI. Other communities felt they could be as well.

For each community, the path was different. The municipalities of Harlingen and Sweetwater owned the land, which comprised the US Air Force bases in those locales. After JCTI established a mobile laboratory in Harlingen, the city deeded portions of the old air base to the Lower Rio Grande Valley Development Council, which then used the property as a match to secure federal grant funding for a multi-year project to construct a $15 million campus. Eventually, the council deeded the acreage and buildings to the state. Sweetwater used a combination of state funding and private foundation dollars for its campus at Avenger Field. Using separate legislative appropriations, the state purchased the land and equipment at the bases in Waco and Amarillo. The key factor

in each case, though, was that community action became the catalyst for a new campus.

Former State Senator Murray Watson, who co-authored the legislation creating JCTI, explained the legislature's urgency regarding technical education during the 1960s and 1970s. "We recognized in Austin that there was a shortage of qualified personnel in the technical workforce. We had always depended upon the military for a trained workforce, but that was changing." High schools no longer emphasized vocational or technical education, and communities began to see TSTI as a lifeline to local economic development and workforce demand.

The lawmakers' interest in a trained workforce for Texas, each community's need for new economic development, and the large number of base closures served as a perfect storm of events to grow JCTI and then TSTI during the institute's first decade.

Subsequent years solidified the need for community support to create new TSTI campuses.

By the time the City of Marshall approached the legislature for a campus, the mood had shifted in Austin, and the effort faced opposition on multiple fronts. Toward the end of the 1980s, not only was the legislature reluctant to create new TSTI campuses, many favored dissolving TSTI altogether and growing the state's network of community colleges.

According to Connie Ware, then chairman of the Marshall Chamber of Commerce, the demographics in East Texas showed a demonstrated, unmet need for technical education. "We had the student population, and we had a huge economic and humanitarian need here for technical workers."

Community leaders traveled by bus to tour the TSTI Waco campus and came back "fired up." They visited other TSTI campuses and studied the range of options. By a wide margin, Marshall passed an additional sales tax for economic development to support the campus. "We would meet twice a week. People traveled to Austin on their own dime, and we did this for years," said Ware. "I've never seen the community come together like it did for TSTI—not even for football!"

Marshall's community leaders worked through several legislative sessions, but finally convinced the legislature of the merits of their cause. In 1991, the same year the legislature changed TSTI's name to Texas State Technical College (TSTC), the legislature passed Senate Bill 1357, authorizing the Marshall campus as an extension center.

The pattern Marshall established continues today. New campuses, as well as partnerships with other educational institutions and industry, are most often initiated by local community action.

Senator Watson, who has remained involved with TSTC in the years following his legislative service, points to recent partnerships in metropolitan areas as a positive next step. "I believe we are on the lip of the cup where we can really go forward. With all the increase in technology, people have to have a skill in today's market." Past and present, regardless of the number of campuses, TSTC's mission is to teach skills and to build the state's workforce. History has shown it takes active, committed communities to get it done.

Senator Watson served in the Texas Legislature for sixteen years, ten of which were in the Senate. His work covered a broad range of issues to include insurance reform, regulation of loan sharks, and the establishment of the Texas Rehabilitation Commission as an independent state agency. He is also responsible for creating the Texas Ranger Hall of Fame, the Temple Medical School as a part of Texas A&M University, and the Tuition Equalization Program.

Upon leaving the legislature, Watson served as TSTC's general counsel for twenty-six years. In 1999, TSTC Waco renamed the campus recreation center in his honor as a tribute to the senator's leadership and on-going support for TSTC. Today, the Murray Watson Jr. Student Recreation Center stands across Campus Drive from one of the Waco campus's newest buildings, the Greta W. Watson Culinary Arts Center, which the Watsons helped to build.

Beginning of Harlingen Campus

Largely because of its early focus on bilingual education and the migrant population, the Harlingen campus benefitted from federal funds through the Economic Development Administration (EDA), an agency within the US Department of Commerce which provides grants to economically distressed communities to generate and/or retain jobs and to stimulate industrial and commercial growth. According to Dr. J. Gilbert Leal, the campus's long-time president, EDA grants assisted with the construction of 90 percent of Harlingen's instructional buildings.

Lieutenant Governor Preston Smith holds a framed rendering of plans for the Harlingen campus.

September 1967
James Connally Technical Institute (JCTI) announces plans for the state's first bilingual technical institute to be located on the former Harlingen Air Force Base. Classes begin in existing facilities with forty students in welding and farm machinery maintenance. An adult basic education course is also implemented to teach adult migrant and seasonal workers.

April 1968
Harlingen branch campus receives a federal grant for $1.905 million following a donation from the city of land and facilities, valued at $1.27 million.

1967

March 1968
Governor John B. Connally requests $2.4 million in federal funds for first-year support for a bilingual technical campus in Harlingen and a $9 million commitment toward a five-year growth plan.

April 13, 1968
State Senator Chet Brooks, chairman of the Texas Senate's Vocational-Technical Education Committee, holds a committee hearing in Harlingen. Representatives from Brownsville voice opposition to a technical school in Harlingen. Mayor George Young of Harlingen refutes opposition and states support for school.

Expansion to Multiple Campuses

Homer K. Taylor

A simple trip to a local optometrist in 1968 became the catalyst for James Connally Technical Institute's (JCTI) fourth campus, located just outside of Sweetwater.

Nolan County's initial efforts to collaborate with adjacent Mitchell and Scurry Counties in order to secure a higher education facility for the area had failed. The failure was largely because the three counties could not agree on where the facility should be located. Each of the counties wanted the school within its own borders.

That is when Homer K. Taylor went to see Dr. John Bowen. Taylor, then assistant principal at Sweetwater High School, had been tasked by his boss to serve on a citizens' committee focused on the higher education issue. During his eye exam, Bowen told Taylor about a friend's son who had recently graduated from JCTI in Waco. After initiating a telephone dialogue with JCTI's administrators, meetings soon followed. Within the month, Bowen and Taylor traveled to Waco to discuss locating a campus in Sweetwater.

With Avenger Field slated for closure by the end of 1969, efforts focused on repurposing the airfield, which was leased by the US Air Force but owned by the City of Sweetwater. Taylor and John Henry "Jack" Kultgen soon contacted the Department of Defense in Albuquerque, New Mexico, and began discussions. The buildings and land were to revert back to Sweetwater, but Kultgen and Taylor also wanted all expendable property and furniture. In a meeting in Sweetwater, the four-star general tasked with the negotiations soundly rejected the idea.

Calling him "the most powerful individual I've ever known," Taylor said Kultgen informed the general they would not take "no" for an answer. Within twenty-four hours, an agreement had been reached to purchase all of Avenger Village and all building inventory. The Rolling Plains Technical

Foundation borrowed $100,000 from the JCTI Foundation for the purchase. In 1969, the Texas Legislature separated JCTI from Texas A&M University and renamed it Texas State Technical Institute (TSTI). TSTI's Rolling Plains Campus on the site of the former Avenger Air Field opened in September of 1970 with 101 students and six programs of study. That same year, State Senator Temple Dickson secured a $150,000 line-item appropriation within TSTI's budget for operational expenses for the Rolling Plains Campus.

Kultgen became the first chairman of the TSTI Board of Regents. He is the namesake for the Waco campus's first new building, the J. H. Kultgen Automotive Center.

Taylor became the first assistant general manager at the Rolling Plains Campus; and later, its president. He oversaw the expansion of TSTI in West Texas with the addition of the Abilene and Breckenridge locations in 1985 and 1989, respectively. In 1991, the legislature changed TSTI's name to Texas State Technical College (TSTC). That same year, TSTC's West Texas locations grew to include Brownwood. Taylor was instrumental in many of the behind-the-scenes events and politicking, which brought these campuses into fruition.

Taylor retired in 2005 after nearly thirty-five years serving the TSTC System. Taylor remains in Sweetwater and is currently the president and executive director of the Nolan County Foundation. He continues to be an active supporter of TSTC, and Sweetwater's main campus drive is named in his honor.

1968

May 10, 1968
Harlingen branch campus of JCTI holds its first graduation exercises for twenty students receiving certificates of completion for a twenty-four-week welding course.

July 1968
Programs at JCTI's branch campus in Harlingen grow to include farm equipment mechanics, diesel mechanics, welding, building maintenance, small engine maintenance, machine tool operation, and floor covering mechanics.

October 16, 1968
The Texas Legislature's House Standing Committee on Education holds a public hearing on vocational-technical education, with State Representative George T. Hinson as chairman. The committee's work led to a recommendation to sever JCTI from Texas A&M University.

October 23, 1968
Before a crowd in excess of five thousand, US Vice President Hubert Humphrey dedicates the Rio Grande Campus of JCTI in Harlingen. Also present are US Senator Ralph Yarborough and US Congressman Kika de la Garza.

April 22, 1969
Local leaders form the Sweetwater Study & Survey Committee for the Utilization of Air Base Facilities in order to find a new use for Avenger Field.

Late April 1969
The Sweetwater committee begins discussions in Waco with Dr. Roy Dugger, director of JCTI, about locating a campus at Avenger Field.

1969

Summer 1969
In the second special session of the summer, the 61st Texas Legislature appropriates $3 million for the purchase of the Amarillo Air Force Base for a new JCTI campus location.

September 1969
Following passage of legislation severing JCTI from Texas A&M University, JCTI's name changes to Texas State Technical Institute (TSTI). Dr. Roy Dugger is named president of the TSTI complex, and he names two executive vice presidents and three additional vice presidents to head the James Connally Campus in Waco, the Rio Grande Campus in Harlingen, and the Mid-Continent Campus at Amarillo.

November 1969
The Sweetwater City Commission sends a letter to Governor Preston Smith requesting permission to start a branch of TSTI at Avenger Field.

November 24, 1969
The governor responds to the Sweetwater City Commission citing portions of House Bill 137 from the 61st Legislature and outlining the steps necessary for a TSTI branch campus to be located at Avenger Field. The legislature appropriates $150,000 for operational expenses.

December 18, 1969
The General Services Administration appraises the Amarillo Air Force Base for $3.9 million. TSTI Chairman of the Board of Regents John Henry "Jack" Kultgen refuses to pay the federal government more than $3 million.

January 13, 1970
The TSTI Board of Regents receives approval for the transfer of property and a branch of the Waco campus at Avenger Field.

TEXAS STATE
TECHNICAL
INSTITUTE

MID-CONTINENT CAMPUS

March 1970
The TSTI Board of Regents authorizes the purchase of the Amarillo Air Force Base, minus 169 housing units and 40 percent of the moveable property, for $3 million in state appropriated funds. Governor Preston Smith approves the offer.

Late March 1970
General Dynamics Corporation announces a new government contract to test and modify the F-111 fighter jet on the James Connally Campus.

June 25, 1970
TSTI caps five years of planning and negotiations with a dedication ceremony at the Amarillo Civic Center, where the Mid-Continent Campus officially becomes part of the TSTI network. Nearly one thousand people attend the event, including Governor Preston Smith, US Congressman Bob Price, the TSTI Board of Regents, state legislators, and other federal, state, and local dignitaries.

March 2, 1970
James Connally Campus breaks ground on the J. H. Kultgen Automotive Technology Center, the first new building to be constructed on campus.

April 3, 1970
TSTI holds groundbreaking ceremonies for the Sweetwater branch campus with Speaker of the Texas House Gus Mutcher attending.

June 22, 1970
TSTI begins its first courses in Amarillo under the auspices of the Manpower Training Act.

The Texas State Technical Institute sign goes up on the Texas Bank Building in advance of opening a campus in Sweetwater.

The Harlingen campus completes the first phase of its massive construction project.

Texas State Technical Institute

NEWS RELEASE
PUBLIC INFORMATION & NEWS
BLDG. 32-6 OFFICE: 817 799-3611 EXT. 224
WACO, TEXAS 76705

ZACK BELCHER, HOME: 848-4487   SHARON MAYHUGH, HOME: 799-1100

DATE _____

...e million dollar building project was dedicated August 23, 1970,
... Grande Campus of the Texas State Technical Institute in Harlingen.
...ts at the state's only bilingual technical school first attended
... the new buildings on the 22-acre campus in September, 1970.
...ies included in the first phase of the three-part project are
...ldings which house: the administration, library, and book store.
...ing modules make up the center section of the new campus, and an
...assroom building featuring visual aids for auto mechanics
... the cluster. The sixth building is an auto mechanics shop.
...or the project were furnished through a grant by the Economic
... Administration of the U. S. Department of Commerce, in cooperation
...d contributions from the city of Harlingen. The program will
...llion dollars when completed in five years.
... Grande Campus of State Tech is one of four facilities under the
...stitute's multi-campus program. It operated as a mobile
...or one year beginning in September of 1967.

###

1970

July 8, 1970
TSTI opens offices in the Texas Bank Building in Sweetwater with four staff members: D. A. Pevehouse as general manager, Homer K. Taylor as assistant general manager, and two office employees.

August 1970
The lease and purchase agreements with the federal government are finalized for Avenger Field.

August 1970
James Connally Campus holds the first annual graduation ceremonies for TSTI. Dr. J. N. Baker, vice president of the Mid-Continent Campus, is the commencement speaker.

August 23, 1970
Rio Grande Campus dedicates a cluster of six buildings, providing space for administrative offices, a technical library, a bookstore, classrooms, and a shop for automotive technology.

August 31, 1970
TSTI opens the Mid-Continent Campus, which includes 1,567 acres of land, three hundred buildings, a golf course, and 336 houses. Classes begin with 254 students, twelve instructors, and seven programs of study.

September 1970
Enrollment at the Rio Grande Campus grows to 850. The campus now offers twenty-one courses of study and boasts new student housing, recreational facilities, and a technical library.

Governor Preston Smith presents the ceremonial key to John Henry "Jack" Kultgen at the opening of the J. H. Kultgen Automotive Technology Center, the first new building constructed on the Waco campus and still an instructional facility.

A sign goes up announcing plans for the W. R. Poage Land Technology Center. Although buildings were completed for several state agencies within the complex, full build-out of the center was never realized.

September 1, 1970
Rolling Plains Campus in Sweetwater opens as a mobile training facility of TSTI's James Connally Campus with 101 full-time students, fifty evening students, twenty-eight personnel, and seven courses of study.

September 24, 1970
Dedication ceremonies are held at the Rolling Plains Campus with Governor Preston Smith as the keynote speaker. Delays with the General Services Commission and other agencies mean the transfer of Avenger Field to Texas and TSTI has still not occurred.

October 13, 1970
The 50,000-square-foot J. H. Kultgen Automotive Technology Center opens on the James Connally Campus. Keynote speaker is Governor Preston Smith.

December 7, 1970
James Connally Campus holds an open house and reception in honor of US Congressman William R. Poage. Plans are announced for the construction of a complex of buildings on fifteen acres near the north entrance of campus to be called the W. R. Poage Land Technology Center. The complex will include buildings for the Texas Parks & Wildlife Department and the Texas Department of Public Safety.

February 1971
General Dynamics Corporation closes operations on the James Connally Campus.

1971
Rio Grande Campus receives accreditation from the Southern Association of Colleges and Schools.

WADE FORESTER, LEFT, AND LANNY WADLEIGHT
. . . turn first spade of ground for building

Ground Breaking Hailed As Major Growth Step

The Rolling Plains Campus in Sweetwater breaks ground on the Wade Forester Automotive Center, which opened on March 13, 1972.

Image above and right: US President Richard Nixon lands on the Rio Grande Campus in Harlingen.

July 26, 1971
James Connally Campus dedicates the Seed Lab, the first of its kind in the world.

January 1972
TSTI is accepted into the membership of the National Commission on Accrediting.

May 1972
Qualitron Aero signs a five-year lease agreement with the James Connally Campus to occupy the former General Dynamics facility.

1971

May 13, 1971
The 62nd Legislature passes House Bill 672, which finally authorizes a TSTI campus in Nolan County and allows for the transfer of Avenger Field to TSTI.

August 2, 1971
Rolling Plains Campus holds its first commencement ceremony with forty-five graduates.

March 13, 1972
Rolling Plains Campus dedicates its first newly constructed building, the Wade Forester Automotive Center, on the former radar installation. Forester was instrumental in the creation of the campus.

Scheherazade Perkins

A 1974 graduate of the chemical technology program, Scheherazade "Sherry" Perkins was directed to Texas State Technical Institute (TSTI) by her father, Luther Mitchell, who was a physics instructor at the Waco campus. "He recognized that TSTI was producing graduates with marketable skills, and he did not feel that the program I was pursuing was a good fit for me or that I would be employed at the end of four years." As it turned out, IBM hired Perkins even before she graduated, and she spent thirty years with the company. "There was nothing at IBM I wasn't prepared for. At TSTI, we were introduced to everything industry had and then some," says Perkins. Although she has left the chemical laboratory and moved into executive positions, Perkins remains a fan of technical education. "Most of us have multiple careers. The key is to identify core passions. That's not just one thing; it may be five or six. Then, identify which one will be self-sustaining—which one will take care of self and family." Perkins is now vice president of Enterprise Solutions Consulting for Profiles International, holds two advanced degrees, and is completing her doctoral dissertation.

June 1974
Dr. Roy Dugger resigns his position as the first system president for TSTI and accepts an appointment as president emeritus.

Summer 1975
Rolling Plains Campus sees significant gains in the number of graduates, with 446 graduating from one-year programs and 1,494 graduating from shorter, specialized courses.

September 22, 1972
US President Richard Nixon visits the Rio Grande Campus.

September 5, 1974
Rolling Plains Campus opens its third new building—a 7,200-square-foot structure containing lab and instructional areas for the building construction craftsmen students.

Dr. Elton E. Stuckly Jr.

Ten years after Texas State Technical College (TSTC) opened its doors as James Connally Technical Institute, one of TSTC's most recognized alumni walked across the stage in Waco to receive his diploma. The year was 1975, and the graduate was Elton E. Stuckly Jr.

Raised in a farming family from the tiny Hill County town of Penelope, Texas, Stuckly was the first in his family to attend college. Describing his father as an excellent farmer with only a seventh grade education, Stuckly said he had little guidance about college or career choices. His first choice was Hill College in Hillsboro, which he left midway through the first semester. He then chose to enroll in Texas State Technical Institute (TSTI).

Explaining he had no clue about a program to select as a field of study, Stuckly perused the school catalog. "I asked myself what program in here was going to be around my entire lifetime." He decided electricity met that criterion. Eighteen months later, Stuckly earned an associate's degree in electrical power technology.

After nearly five years at Fluor Engineering in Houston and another seven years at General Tire & Rubber Company in Waco, Stuckly was back at TSTI—this time as an instructor. Stuckly's career at the college has spanned nearly thirty years and led him to the presidency of TSTC's flagship campus in Waco. Along the way, Stuckly earned both a bachelor of science degree in technology and a master of science degree with emphasis in human resource development from the University of Texas at Tyler, as well as a doctorate in higher education leadership from the University of Mary Hardin-Baylor.

Stuckly's career at TSTC almost never happened. Three and a half hours after he accepted the instructor's job at TSTI, Stuckly received a second offer from the nuclear power plant at Glen Rose, which included more money. Calling the decision a fork in the road, Stuckly felt he was duty-bound to keep his commitment to TSTI.

Although Stuckly calls making the switch from Hill College to TSTI the best thing he ever did, his father thought the decision was a huge mistake. Reflecting upon his own confusion about a career path, Stuckly believes students need to be exposed to as much as possible prior to graduation from high school through dual credit programs and other pathways. Asked about the advice he gives students today, Stuckly said, "Pick something you enjoy doing. Forty to forty-five years is too long to work at something you don't enjoy."

Although he contends that being an instructor is the best job on campus, Stuckly added, "Being president was awesome. I got to do something different every day!"

Eventually, his father agreed Stuckly had made the right choice. When the evening news reported Stuckly's appointment as president of TSTC Waco, his father watched from a favorite living room chair with tears rolling down his face. His son had traversed the gamut from first generation college student, to instructor, to department chairman, to cluster director, to dean of instruction, to vice president of instruction, to college president. In 2014, Stuckly took still another leap in his career at TSTC. He became vice chancellor and chief operations officer for the entire system of TSTC colleges.

Stuckly is the ultimate TSTC success story. Referring to the period when Air Force One landed at TSTC Waco's airfield under US President George W. Bush, Stuckly said, "I am a boy from Penelope, Texas, and I have met heads of state from all over the world." As Stuckly often says, "It just doesn't get any better than that."

(Photo by Marlene S. McMichael)

Harlon Fentress, instrumental in bringing Texas State Technical Institute to Waco, is honored at opening ceremonies for the Harlon M. Fentress Center on the James Connally Campus. Governor Dolph Briscoe (far left) attends the ceremony.

Fifinella was the mascot for the Women Airforce Service Pilots (WASPs) who trained at Avenger Field. The bronze of the mascot is now located in the National WASP World War II Museum in Sweetwater, Texas.

November 20, 1975
Governor Dolph Briscoe participates in the groundbreaking for the Harlon M. Fentress Center on the James Connally Campus.

February 23, 1976
Dr. Roy Dugger resigns as TSTI's president emeritus.

June 14, 1976
Rolling Plains Campus holds ceremonies to unveil a five-foot bronze sculpture of Fifinella, a winged superhero from the book, *The Gremlins* by Roald Dahl, and immortalized by Walt Disney. Fifinella is the mascot for the Women Airforce Service Pilots (WASPs), who trained at Avenger Field in World War II. (Although later moved, the bronze was placed in the "lucky coin fountain" used by the WASPs and still located on campus. It commemorates the WASPs' heroic contributions during the war effort.)

1975

October 1975
Rio Grande Campus sees a 50 percent increase in enrollment.

1976
Rio Grande Campus dedicates the Health Information Technology Building and the Service Support Center.

June 1976
Enrollment at the Rolling Plains Campus tops 1,140 students for summer classes.

TSTI James Connally Campus → **TSTI Waco**

TSTI Rio Grande Campus → **TSTI Harlingen**

TSTI Mid-Continent Campus → **TSTI Amarillo**

TSTI Rolling Plains Campus → **TSTI Sweetwater**

TSTISYSTEM
Texas State Technical Institute

TSTIWACO
Texas State Technical Institute

TSTIHARLINGEN
Texas State Technical Institute

TSTIAMARILLO
Texas State Technical Institute

TSTISWEETWATER
Texas State Technical Institute

1978

February–March 1978
Campus names transition to TSTI Amarillo, TSTI Harlingen, TSTI Sweetwater, and TSTI Waco.

March 14, 1978
Governor Dolph Briscoe visits TSTI Sweetwater while campaigning for a third term as governor.

1979
TSTI Sweetwater receives full accreditation from the Southern Association of Colleges and Schools.

May 1979
TSTI Waco begins construction on new apartments to house up to 224 students.

1980
TSTI Harlingen dedicates the Computer Science Programs Building and the Student Residence Oak Tree.

May 18, 1980
TSTI Sweetwater dedicates the Lance Sears Industrial Technology Center, honoring the former TSTI regent.

Governor Dolph Briscoe greets a student on the Sweetwater campus on March 14, 1978.

Sami Weatherall

In 1981, Sami Peterson Weatherall became the first female graduate in what is now called mechatronics technology at the Harlingen campus. Relating the often-humorous aspects of being in such a non-traditional program, Weatherall says, "Of course, I had to prove a point." She graduated with a 4.0 grade point average and received a standing ovation at graduation from her instructors.

The reason Weatherall enrolled in Texas State Technical Institute (TSTI) is as unusual as was her degree for the decade. "Basically, I was a smart kid who ended up in the wrong room at a high school college night." The TSTI recruiter she met there was "kind of cute," and Weatherall was hooked.

Once the decision was made, "I never had second thoughts about attending TSTI. So many, today, have a preconceived notion that they have to go to a four-year school to get a great job, and it is not so. It is a shame we have a shortage of technically trained workers today. The marine off-shore industry is booming. For trained technicians, there are jobs out there for sure."

Weatherall has used her degree throughout her career in electronics and marine technology, working for huge companies like Dow Chemical Company, Kongserg Maritime, and Schottel Inc. "I have had fun with my jobs. It's been great."

October 22, 1980
US President Jimmy Carter, accompanied by country singer Jerry Jeff Walker, holds a rally at TSTI Waco.

November 19, 1981
TSTI Waco dedicates the Provence Graphic Communications Center, named after long-time editor of the *Waco News-Tribune* and the *Times Herald*, Harry M. Provence.

October 28, 1981
Governor Bill Clements signs deed to lands from the City of Harlingen for TSTI's expansion.

1982
TSTI Amarillo enjoys its all-time peak enrollment of 1,166 students.

The leather works program featuring custom boot making was a popular program on Texas State Technical Institute's Amarillo campus.

May 1982
TSTI Waco holds groundbreaking ceremonies for the Technical Studies Center, the Electrical Trades Center, and the Construction Trades Center.

1983
TSTI Harlingen dedicates the Industrial Trades Building.

May 1983
The 68th Legislature passes House Bill 178, which authorizes TSTI to create extension centers. Originally specific to Hidalgo County, the legislation is amended before final passage to allow TSTI to provide temporary programs across the state to address existing unemployment issues. The legislature provides line-item funding in the appropriations bill for an extension center in McAllen as part of TSTI Harlingen.

1982

1983
TSTI Harlingen dedicates the Administration/ Industrial Technology Building.

1983
Titles for the head administrators on all TSTI campuses change from general manager to president.

June 10, 1983
TSTI Waco holds groundbreaking ceremonies for the Student Services Center.

Sam Sepulveda

Fleet Manager Sam Sepulveda, a 1985 Harlingen graduate in automotive technology, maintains over 2,700 vehicles for the Rio Grande Valley Sector of the United States Customs and Border Patrol. With obvious pride in the education he received at Texas State Technical Institute, Sepulveda says, "Many may not think about it, but we are the doctors of the vehicles on the road. A top notch auto mechanic can get paid good money and be very successful."

Texas State Technical Institute's McAllen campus.

Governor Mark White poses with President J. Gilbert Leal while visiting the Harlingen campus.

July 26, 1983
TSTI Sweetwater dedicates the D. A. Pevehouse Technology Center.

October 15, 1983
Governor Mark White attends the dedication of the Electrical Trades Center & Library and the Technical Studies Center at TSTI Waco.

1985
Governor Mark White uses $370,000 in office funds to open the Abilene Extension Center as part of TSTI Sweetwater.

Fall 1983
TSTI Harlingen opens the McAllen Extension Center.

1985
TSTI Harlingen dedicates the Chemical/ Environmental Technology Building.

February 3, 1985
The first jet airplanes land at the new $6.5 million hangar for Electrospace Systems Inc. on the TSTI Waco airfield.

TSTI counselor Dale McDaniel helps out with remodeling

Larry Lawrence/Reporter-News

Classes to start Thursday at TSTI Abilene extension

By LARRY LAWRENCE

Business Editor

m-2-24-85

It may not look much like a college campus, but the Abilene extension of Texas State Technical Institute is about ready to start registration and classes.

Registration will open Monday and continue through Wednesday for the spring quarter, and classes will start Thursday. Registration will be from 9 a.m. to 8 p.m. Monday, and from 8 a.m. to 5 p.m. on other days.

The building — the old Lankford Manufacturing Co. facility at 2041 S. Second St. — has been undergoing an interior transformation since plans for the extension were announced Jan. 9. It's been a do-it-yourself operation in most respects, as staff and designated faculty members pitched in to help with the facelift.

"Everyone has been pitching in to get the building ready for classes," said Gerald Schwalb, director of special projects who has charge of the center. While a lot of work remains to be done on the 22,000-square-foot building, things will be in shape for the opening of classes, Schwalb assured prospective students.

Schwalb, a retired Air Force lieutenant colonel, said all the necessary equipment, machines and material needed for classes will be in place and ready for the first students Thursday.

Much of the heavy equipment for the production machine operator course is in place. That course was added to the curriculum after the announcement that an extension of the Sweetwater technical school would be

Larry Lawrence/Reporter-News

Gerald Schwalb — Heads TSTI extension

opened in Abilene.

The only course longer than 12 weeks is basic electricity and electronics. It requires 36 weeks for a certificate or 18 months for an associate degree, with the first half taught in Abilene and the last 36 weeks in Sweetwater.

The other three courses being offered are automated office technician, emergency medical technician and medical record clerk transcriptionist. Each of these, and the machine operator program, is 12 weeks with completion of each leading to certification.

One of the major tasks in preparing the building for use by TSTI was that of constructing six classrooms, including the laboratory for the electronics course. The building basically was one huge room and one smaller one when it was last used.

Schwalb and other staff members have been doing most of the construction themselves, and they were busy Friday morning preparing classroom walls for painting. As the former officer noted, everyone seemed willing to do whatever work they could to speed the project along.

"We have space to build five or six more classrooms, which would allow us to double our capacity," Schwalb said. "Hopefully, we will be able to add some more subjects in September. We are planning to grow."

The construction currently under way should accommodate about 200 students in the five technical programs. The curriculum is designed to provide schooling in areas of technical training not being covered by other local technical training facilities.

At present the extension has a five-member administrative staff, including Schwalb, and instructors named to three of the five courses. All of the courses will have instructors assigned by the time classes open.

On the staff are Dale McDaniel, student counselor; Sheila J. Richie, clerk; Julia D. Griffin, accountant, and Sheila M. Middleton, secretary.

All three of the instructors already named were transferred from the Sweetwater TSTI main campus to Abilene. John Young of Abilene is instructor for the electronics classes; Vernon Wade of Merkel will teach the emergency medical technician course; and Sam Hanley, also of Abilene, is the automated office technical instructor.

"Right now we have a minimal amount of furniture and a lot more work to do to make the building look like we want it to," Schwalb said. "But all our teaching materials will be on hand to start classes."

Automotive Technology Named Top Training Program in U.S.

TSTI-Waco's Automotive Technology program has been named national winner of the American Vocational Association's 1986 Award for Excellence in Automotive Service Programs for postsecondary schools.

"This is the top award in the country for automotive training programs," Program Chairman Henry Brooks said. "I don't know what we'll do for an encore."

The award is co-sponsored by the Industry Planning Council of the Motor Vehicle Manufacturer's Association. The council is made up of representatives of major automobile manufacturers, members of the automotive service industry, and vocational educators.

TSTI-Waco's Automotive Technology program was recognized as the outstanding training program in the state last June, Brooks said. The state-level honor qualified the program to be considered for the AVA's national award.

For the national competition, AUT submitted an 832-page self study which covered topics such as curriculum and course descriptions, advisory committee, instructional resources, placement, facilities, instructors' qualifications, and program accomplishments.

The program will officially receive the award at the closing general session AVA's national convention in Dallas. The session will be held at the Loew's Anatole Hotel at 3:30 p.m. on Dec. 9.

An award of $1,000 will be given to AUT to reimburse the costs of attending the convention. The program also will receive equipment and curriculum materials to be used for instructional purposes.

1986
TSTI Waco's automotive technology program is named the country's top automotive training program and is the national winner of the American Vocational Association's 1986 Award for Excellence in Automotive Service Programs for post-secondary schools.

February 28, 1985
Abilene Extension Center opens with five programs of study in a building on South Second Street, once occupied by the Lankford Manufacturing Company.

June 14, 1985
Governor Mark White signs Senate Bill 911.

1985

May 27, 1985
The 69th Legislature passes Senate Bill 911 placing TSTI under the sole authority of the Coordinating Board, Texas College and University System (the precursor to the Texas Higher Education Coordinating Board) and removing it from the authority of the Texas Education Agency.

1986
Combined enrollment for all TSTI campuses reaches nearly 8,800 students and ninety programs of study at campuses in Amarillo, Harlingen, Sweetwater, and Waco, as well as the two extension centers in Abilene and McAllen.

1986
TSTI Harlingen dedicates the Annex Building and the Palo Blanco Dormitory.

Fall 1986
Enrollment at TSTI Harlingen and its McAllen Extension Center reaches more than 2,500 students in regular programs.

Fall 1986
Enrollment reaches 4,722 at TSTI Waco.

January 1987
US Senator Phil Gramm dedicates the Short Course Center at TSTI Harlingen.

1988
TSTI Harlingen holds groundbreaking for a new facility for the building systems technology program.

June 1986
TSTI Waco hosts the Texas Air Expo, a five-day event celebrating the state's 150th birthday and featuring the Texas National Guard F-4 team, the Concorde airliner, a World War II Douglas A-20, and the Goodyear Blimp.

1987
TSTI Waco ranks first among the state's seventy-seven two-year college campuses in both certificates awarded and vocational degrees awarded, with over five times more degrees awarded than the state average of 177.

February 1987
US Congressman Kika de la Garza opens the third building at the McAllen Extension Center.

Robbie the Robot

Robbie was used throughout the 1990s by the electrical department on the Waco campus to add some "tech" fun to campus functions and special events. Robbie became a top recruiter for the college. The Texas Department of Public Safety donated Robbie the Robot to Texas State Technical College.

September 1, 1988
The TSTI Board of Regents adopts Minute Order 79-88, which changes the title of the head administrator of the TSTI system from president to chancellor.

Spring 1989
The 71st Legislature provides funding in the appropriations bill for a rural technology center at Breckenridge as part of TSTI Sweetwater.

September 20, 1990
TSTI Sweetwater holds opening ceremonies for its new Breckenridge Extension Center.

1988

December 1988
The Motor Vehicle Manufacturers Association names TSTI Waco's automotive technology program the "Best in State."

1990
TSTI Harlingen holds a groundbreaking for a new student center.

September 6, 1990
Classes begin with ninety-five students and seven courses of study at the Breckenridge Extension Center, part of TSTI Sweetwater.

United in Goal for Campus

Community support turned opposition in the legislature to create the Marshall campus for Texas State Technical College (TSTC). "Republicans and Democrats do not always work together, but citizens crossed party lines and supported this campus because of a common belief that it was good for the town," said Tony Williams, who was the city manager for Marshall in 1991. "The sentiment in the community is still absolutely positive. TSTC Marshall is widely recognized by the community as one of those good things Marshall has going for it—but not just Marshall, the whole area."

1991
Breckenridge Extension Center holds its first capping ceremony for eleven vocational nursing students.

May 27, 1991
The 72nd Legislature passes Senate Bill 1357 by State Senator Bill Ratliff, establishing the Marshall Extension Center and providing funding for the center in the appropriations bill.

January 22, 1991
TSTI celebrates its twenty-fifth anniversary in Austin.

May 1991
The 72nd Legislature provides funding in the appropriations bill for the Brownwood Extension Center as part of TSTI Sweetwater.

Summer 1991
TSTI Harlingen dedicates the Student Center, which includes a cafeteria and bookstore.

Bill renames TSTI as a college system

By DEBBIE GRAVES
Cox News Service

AUSTIN — The Texas State Technical Institute System will get a new name under legislation given tentative approval by the House Friday.

The House, however, delayed at least until Monday action on another bill that would create a TSTI extension center in Marshall.

In approving the broader bill by state Rep. Ashley Smith, R-Houston, state representatives agreed to changing the name of the TSTI system to the Texas State Technical College System. The name change is designed to clear up confusion among college-age students who sometimes think TSTI is simply a trade or business school.

This legislation cleared the House with no debate Friday. Once the House gives the bill final approval early next week, the bill will go to Gov. Ann Richards for her consideration.

Along with changing the name, Smith's bill would:

• Allow the system's board of regents to purchase land in any county in which TSTI has a campus. This provision is a reaction to a state audit that questioned the legality of the TSTI regents' purchase of a house in Waco for the system's chancellor in 1988.

• Creates a formal procedure for the system to follow when adding new schools to the system.

• Gives the board of regents eminent domain powers, which means the school could foreclose on property if the land or building was needed by the school.

• Authorizes TSTI-Waco to operate its existing airport as a public airport, which makes it eligible for grants and funding from the Federal Aviation Administration.

Another bill to establish a TSTI branch in Marshall was scheduled for debate by the House on Friday. The legislation by state Rep. Paul Sadler, D-Henderson, was placed on the calendar for uncontested bills but it ran into last-minute opposition.

TSTI Waco → **TSTC Waco**

TSTI Harlingen → **TSTC Harlingen**

TSTI Amarillo → **TSTC Amarillo**

TSTI Sweetwater → **TSTC Sweetwater**

1991

September 1, 1991
With the passage of Senate Bill 1222 by the 72nd Legislature, TSTI's name changes to Texas State Technical College (TSTC). Campus names change to TSTC Waco, TSTC Harlingen, TSTC Amarillo, and TSTC Sweetwater.

September 1, 1991
TSTC Waco opens the Marshall Extension Center, also known as the TSTC East Texas Center.

Mid-September 1991
The TSTC Board of Regents approves the establishment of the Brownwood Extension Center.

Mid-September 1991
TSTC Harlingen and the University of Texas at San Antonio sign an articulation agreement facilitating student transfers for bachelor's degrees in science and engineering.

Gregoria Arellano Jr.

A self-described troublemaker and poor student in school, Gregoria Arellano Jr. says he was "bitten by the education bug" at Texas State Technical Institute (TSTI) in Harlingen. While earning a degree in drafting and design technology in 1991, he found he was able to apply what he was learning in his design projects. "I saw the purpose of education, and that gave me a taste of who I really was as an individual." The experience flipped a switch for Arellano, who went on to earn two additional degrees from the University of Texas Pan American.

Arellano never worked as a draftsman. Instead, he found he loved teaching. Arellano is now the principal at Rivas Elementary School in the Donna Independent School District. "Technical education opened a door and allowed me to believe that I could do it. TSTI gave me a stepping stone to where I am now."

Mid-September 1991
TSTC Harlingen pilots the Tech Prep Program with high schools in Harlingen, San Benito, and Weslaco. The campus also begins the College Connection Program, allowing high school students to take courses on campus.

Fall 1991
TSTC Harlingen dedicates the Wellness and Sports Center.

December 1991
McAllen Extension Center dedicates the Learning Resource Center.

September 27, 1991
Having outgrown its first facility, the Abilene Extension Center holds a ribbon cutting and open house at its new location on East Highway 80.

Fall 1991
The TSTC star becomes the new, iconic logo for TSTC.

December 12, 1991
TSTC Waco becomes part of the new Mid-Coast Higher Education Consortium intended to provide programs in chemical technology, environmental technology, and aquaculture/marine technology at the Palacios Marine Education Center.

The ribbon is cut on the George F. Young Engineering Technology Building on the Harlingen campus. As mayor, Young was instrumental in bringing Texas State Technical College to Harlingen.

March 1992
The TSTC Board of Regents approves the Mid-Coast Higher Education Consortium agreement and authorizes instructional programs at Palacios.

Summer 1992
Brownwood Extension Center opens with thirteen employees and seven programs of study.

1993
Marshall Extension Center holds classes in the North Campus, a former Gibson's store.

1992

Summer 1992
Harlingen is named an "All American City," partially due to TSTC's strong presence in the community.

August 1992
Marshall Extension Center holds its first classes in temporary quarters in the Marshall Exploration Building.

May 14, 1993
TSTC Harlingen dedicates the George F. Young Engineering Technology Building.

Retiring State Senator Temple Dickson and his wife cut the ribbon on the R. Temple Dickson Center for Engineering Technologies on the Sweetwater campus. Many dignitaries attended the event. Pictured are State Senator Bill Sims (left) and State Representative David Counts (right).

May 22, 1993
Governor Ann Richards and US Attorney General Janet Reno visit TSTC Sweetwater for the fiftieth anniversary of the Women Airforce Service Pilots, who lived and trained on the Sweetwater campus.

August 30, 1993
Under Senate Bill 251, the McAllen Extension Center separates from TSTC and becomes a new community college, known today as South Texas Community College.

September 9, 1993
TSTC Waco opens the Aerospace Technologies Center.

July 19, 1993
Community College Week ranks TSTC Harlingen as the number one producer of Hispanic graduates in engineering-related technologies among two-year schools. TSTC Waco ranks number two.

September 1993
TSTC Harlingen breaks ground on new student housing.

September 23, 1993
TSTC Sweetwater dedicates the R. Temple Dickson Center for Engineering Technologies. Formerly a state representative and then a state senator, Dickson was instrumental in obtaining state and federal support for the campus.

The City of Harlingen serves as the "Texas Capital for a Day."

1993

Fall 1993
TSTC Waco begins offering evening classes in Palacios.

1994
TSTC Harlingen opens the Las Palmas Dormitory.

September 1994
TSTC Waco completes construction on the Student Recreation Center.

1994
Enrollment at TSTC Amarillo declines to 536 students, capping steady declines since 1986 which were accompanied by corresponding reductions in funding and program offerings.

July 28, 1994
Governor Ann Richards and three state agencies conduct state business on campus at TSTC Harlingen when the city is chosen to serve as the "Capital for a Day."

November 1, 1994
TSTC Harlingen dedicates the Aviation Maintenance Technology Building, a 45,000-square-foot facility.

The first building on the Marshall Extension Center's new "South" Campus begins to take shape. The ribbon was cut to open the building in July 1996.

1995
Marshall Extension Center begins construction on a new "South" Campus with $5.4 million in funds from the Economic Development Administration and the Marshall Economic Development Corporation, placing the total investment in TSTC's East Texas extension center at over $11 million.

May 17, 1995
The 74th Legislature passes House Bill 2507, authorizing the TSTC Board of Regents to transfer TSTC Amarillo to Amarillo College.

December 17, 1996
TSTC Harlingen dedicates the Senator Eddie Lucio Health Science Technology Building.

Summer 1995
TSTC Harlingen signs a Tech Prep agreement with Brownsville and Harlingen school districts for automated manufacturing technology.

July 1996
Marshall Extension Center dedicates its new 80,000-square-foot facility, the first on the new South Campus.

1997
Marshall Extension Center offers on-campus housing for one hundred students. The Marshall Higher Education Financing Corporation provides funding for the project.

Texas Governor
George Bush visits
TSTC Sweewater's
Class 1000
Clean Room

January 20, 1998
Governor George W. Bush attends the dedication of TSTC Sweetwater's semiconducting clean room.

1999
Breckenridge Extension Center celebrates its tenth anniversary with an open house and a new facility, the Rick Perry Higher Education Center.

April 30, 1999
TSTC Waco dedicates the new Transportation Technologies Center.

1998

September 1998
TSTC Harlingen dedicates the Science and Technology Building.

January 26, 1999
TSTC Sweetwater holds groundbreaking ceremonies for a new student housing complex.

June 19, 1999
Governor George W. Bush signs House Bill 1049 authorizing the Marshall Extension Center to become a stand-alone college under the TSTC system.

The Waco campus's John B. Connally Technology Center.

November 1999
TSTC Harlingen dedicates the Early Childhood Development Center.

2000
TSTC Harlingen dedicates the Agricultural Technology Building.

January 27, 2000
TSTC Harlingen dedicates the Autobody Collision Technology Building.

November 5, 1999
TSTC Waco opens the John B. Connally Technology Center, with Idanell "Nellie" Connally, the widow of Governor Connally, in attendance.

2000
TSTC Sweetwater opens four new student housing units, called the Pecan, Mesquite, Oak, and Cedar Lodges.

2001
TSTC Sweetwater opens a new bookstore, called Tex-Books & More, as well as an additional student housing facility, called the Bluebonnet Inn.

Dr. and Mrs. Elton E. Stuckly Jr. greet US President George W. Bush following Air Force One's landing at Waco's airport. The Texas State Technical College airport was used whenever President Bush flew to his Texas ranch. (Photo courtesy of Dr. Stuckly)

January 26, 2001
TSTC Harlingen dedicates the Semiconductor Manufacturing Building.

August 29, 2001
After serving seven American presidents and carrying US President George W. Bush and First Lady Laura Bush, Air Force One No. 27000 lands at TSTC Waco's airport on its last flight before being retired.

February 8, 2002
The TSTC Board of Regents adopts a new expanded statement of purpose for TSTC Harlingen, as required by the Southern Association of Colleges and Schools.

2001

August 2001
TSTC Waco begins partnership with Wharton County Junior College to offer courses in Richmond.

2002
TSTC Marshall receives full accreditation from the Southern Association of Colleges and Schools.

December 2002
TSTC Harlingen kicks off the College for Texans Campaign, a statewide campaign to raise awareness about the benefits of going to college.

TEXAS HIGHER EDUCATION COORDINATING BOARD
P.O. Box 12788 Austin, Texas 78711

October 24, 2005

Robert W. Shepard
CHAIRMAN
Neal W. Adams
VICE CHAIRMAN
Vacant
SECRETARY OF THE BOARD

Laurie Bricker
Jerry Farrington
Paul Foster
George L. McWilliams
Nancy R. Neal
Lorraine Perryman
Lyn Bracewell Phillips
Curtis Ransom
A. W. "Whit" Riter III

William Segura
Chancellor
Texas State Technical College System
3801 Campus Drive
Waco, TX 76705

Dear Chancellor Segura:

I am responding to your letter of August 2, 2005 in which you request permission for Texas State Technical College (TSTC)-Harlingen to participate in

Chancellor Segura
October 24, 2005
Page 2

and helps students gain increased intellectual skills and knowledge, making them more "well-rounded" students. Finally, Coordinating Board staff will monitor developments in South Texas and if necessary, reconsider this decision, to ensure that this change in practice does not inhibit the ability of nearby institutions of higher education to fulfill their missions.

This decision makes it even more important that TSTC-Harlingen expand its working relationships with both Texas Southmost College and South Texas College. I know you and Dr. Gilbert Leal, President of TSTC-Harlingen, will work closely with Presidents Garcia and Reed to coordinate your activities.

We continue to discover that the challenge of successfully meeting the *Closing the Gaps* goals often leads us to revisit long-held beliefs and operating rules. I look forward to continuing to work with you on this and related higher education initiatives.

Sincerely,

Dear Chancellor Segura:

I am responding to your letter of August 2, 2005 in which you request permission for Texas State Technical College (TSTC)-Harlingen to participate in statewide core curriculum requirements. I approve your request with the condition these courses are offered only at the TSTC-Harlingen campus for the sole purpose of providing transferable courses to area students seeking baccalaureate degrees.

courses are readily available from other Texas higher education institutions via distance learning. She raised issues regarding statutory authority and Southern Association of Colleges and Schools Level I accreditation. Finally, she expressed concern that expanding the role of TSTC-Harlingen to that of a public community college without the local community commitment to provide a property tax would negatively impact the surrounding communities in potential plans to create a local community college.

Given Dr. Reed's concerns, I want to re-iterate several points. First, this decision applies only to the Harlingen campus. No other region of the state faces the unique set of circumstances and demand as found in South Texas. Second, your proposal provides the state additional higher education resources to help meet the goals of *Closing the Gaps*. Making the full core curriculum available to Harlingen-area residents promotes a college-going culture, a culture of transfer,

AN EQUAL OPPORTUNITY EMPLOYER

Greg Sowell

According to Greg Sowell, a 2002 computer science graduate from Texas State Technical College (TSTC), "Why waste time?" Sowell knew what he wanted to pursue as a career. "Technical schools like TSTC provide a faster time to market. By the time the four-year graduates showed up, I had two years of work experience on them." Sowell is the engineering director for three data centers for FIBERTOWN, a Texas-based data center, co-location, and disaster recovery services provider. He also provides consulting services for a wide range of clients, including the Memphis Grizzlies, a national basketball team. "Students should focus on what they want to do and go directly to it." Great pay and less school debt are only part of the reward.

December 2002
TSTC Harlingen opens the ACT Center, which offers employee training for local businesses.

January 22, 2004
TSTC Harlingen dedicates the Learning Resource Center and celebrates Dr. J. Gilbert Leal's twenty-fifth year as president.

2005
The Texas Higher Education Coordinating Board grants approval for TSTC Harlingen to teach the academic core, making it the only TSTC campus to do so.

October 2003
TSTC Harlingen renames the Science and Technology Building after State Representative Irma Rangel.

September 2004
TSTC Sweetwater opens the Transportation Technologies Center.

December 4, 2006
TSTC Sweetwater launches its wind energy and turbine technology program with classes to begin in the spring semester.

2008
TSTC Harlingen dedicates the Cultural Arts Center.

October 2008
TSTC Waco achieves ranking by American Culinary Federation.

November 2008
The TSTC Board of Regents formally accepts the Brownwood property.

2006

August 15, 2007
Under House Bill 2074 by the 80th Legislature, TSTC Waco and Temple College sign a partnership agreement for a new multi-institution higher education center to be located in Taylor and called the East Williamson County Higher Education Center.

July 2008
TSTC Sweetwater completes major renovations to two of its main buildings, the D. A. Pevehouse Technology Center and the Lance Sears Industrial Technology Center.

October 2008
The City of Brownwood and the Brownwood Economic Development Corporation transfer the title to three downtown buildings to TSTC.

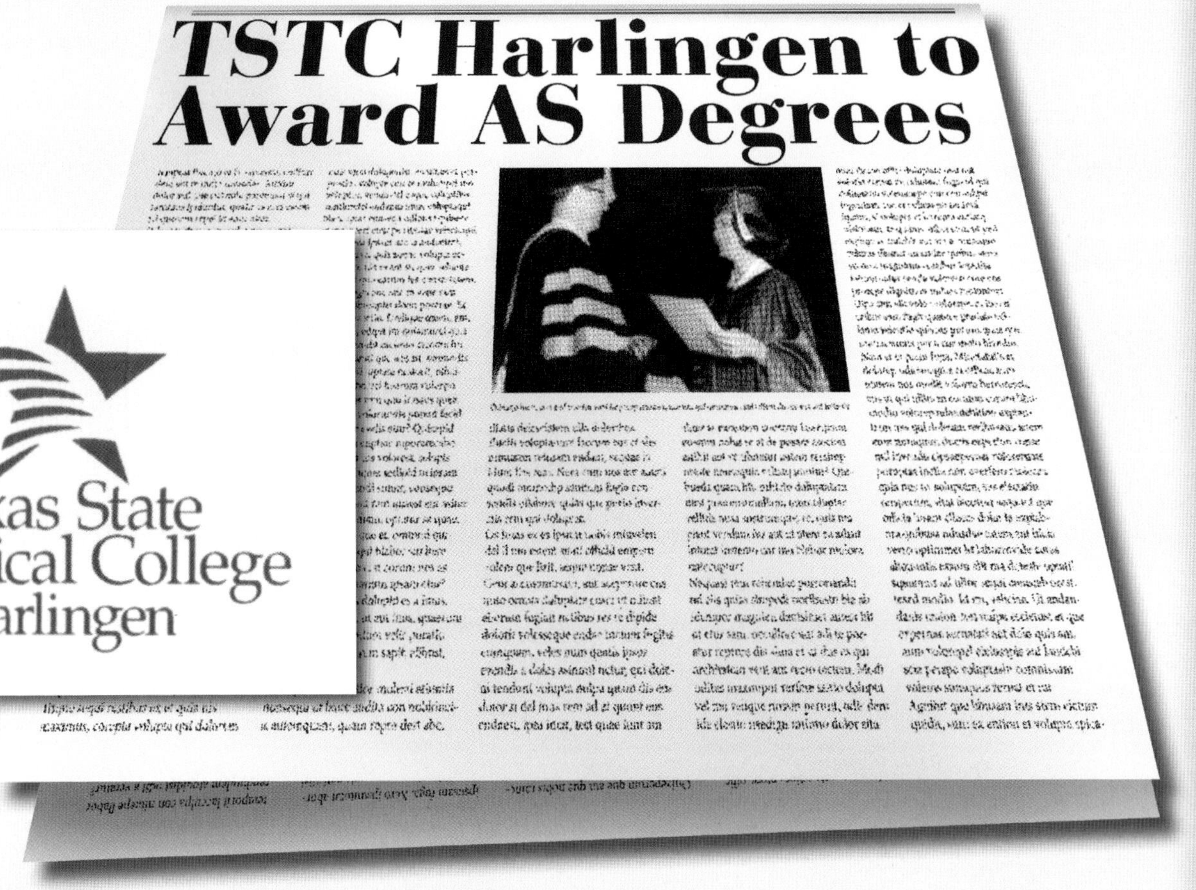

Texas State
Technical College
Harlingen

Dr. J. Gilbert Leal

Harlingen's Learning Resource Center was renamed in honor of Dr. J. Gilbert Leal on May 29, 2009. Leal began his career at Texas State Technical College (TSTC) as an instructor in 1969 when the college was called Texas State Technical Institute. He retired in 2008, after serving as Harlingen's general manager and president for thirty years. It was a tenure which made him the longest serving head administrator at any TSTC campus. Leal oversaw the campus's growth from a fledgling institution of twenty-five acres to a sprawling 160-acre facility. Harlingen is the only TSTC campus which teaches the academic core curriculum and awards associate of science degrees.

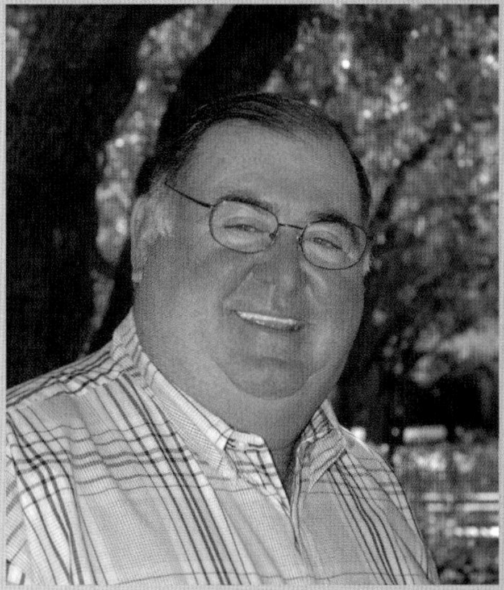

Dr. J. Gilbert Leal, General Manager/ President, Harlingen campus, 1978–2008

2009
Breckenridge Extension Center celebrates its twentieth anniversary and honors retiring provost Burrell McKelvain.

May 29, 2009
TSTC Harlingen holds a ceremony honoring President J. Gilbert Leal and changing the name of the Learning Resource Center to the Dr. J. Gilbert Leal Learning Resource Center.

June 19, 2009
Governor Rick Perry signs House Bill 1325 granting TSTC Harlingen the authority to grant associate of science degrees. The legislation made Harlingen the only campus with the authority to award the transferable degrees. Traditionally, TSTC awards associate of applied science degrees.

August 2009
The Texas Education Agency designates Rapoport Academy as an Early College High School partner with TSTC Waco through the Texas High School Project.

August 27, 2009
TSTC Marshall receives the Technical Education Award from the Coordination and Development Corporation.

Governor Rick Perry greets students on the Waco campus in advance of his December press conference.

October 2, 2009
TSTC Waco renames the Aerospace Technologies Center in honor of the school's first director, Dr. Roy Dugger, who attends the ceremony.

2010
TSTC Marshall and Encore Multimedia receive the 2010 MarCom Gold Award for their "Veterans' TV Spot."

April 10, 2010
The Federal Aviation Administration grants approval for the air traffic control program (ATC) at TSTC Waco, making it the only public college in Texas to offer ATC training.

2009

December 2009
Governor Rick Perry visits TSTC Waco to announce a new initiative to enhance high-tech education.

March 4, 2010
TSTC Waco breaks ground on a golf course and landscape management facility.

May 3, 2010
TSTC Waco breaks ground on the Colonel James T. Connally Aerospace Center.

Dr. Roy Dugger

"No person was ever honored for what he received.
Honor has been the reward for what he gave."
—*Calvin Coolidge, 30th President of the United States, 1872-1933*

Dr. Roy Dugger Center
Building Dedication Ceremony
Texas State Technical College Waco
October 2, 2009

Welcome . . . . Mr. Rob Wolaver
Executive Vice President

TSTC "The Beginning" . . . . Mr. Elton E. Stuckly, Jr.
President

Recognition of Platform Guests . . . Mr. Stuckly

Proclamation . . . . Ms. Virginia DuPuy
Mayor, City of Waco

Words of Gratitude &
Introduction of Honoree . . . . Dr. Bill Segura
Chancellor

Honoree Remarks . . . . Dr. Roy Dugger

Unveiling & Conclusion . . . . Mr. Wolaver

Technical education
visionary—Dr. Roy Dugger

June 26, 2010
TSTC Sweetwater signs an agreement with
Breckenridge officials to expand the campus
for the Breckenridge Extension Center.

Summer 2010
TSTC Waco closes the Palacios location.

Fall 2010
Abilene Extension Center becomes home to
Abilene Independent School District's magnet high
school—the Academy for Technology, Engineering,
Math, and Science, known as ATEMS.

2011
TSTC Marshall and Encore Multimedia receive the 2011 MarCom
Honorable Mention Award for their "Updating Status TV Spot."

2011
TSTC Marshall and Encore Multimedia receive the 2011
MarCom Platinum Award for their "Before and After TV Spot."

January 2011
TSTC West Texas is one of the first to earn the American
Wind Energy Association's Seal of Approval for its wind
turbine service technician program.

The Waco campus announces plans for the new Greta W. Watson Culinary Arts Center. Pictured with President Elton E. Stuckly Jr. and Chef Mark Schneider are Mrs. Watson and former State Senator Murray Watson Jr.

February 10, 2011
TSTC Waco breaks ground on a new culinary arts center.

June 29, 2011
State Representative Susan King passes a resolution honoring TSTC West Texas for being named among the top 120 community colleges in the nation by the Aspen Institute.

August 2011
TSTC Waco announces a $1 million pledge from the Brazos Higher Education Service Corporation for the new culinary arts center to be named the Greta W. Watson Culinary Arts Center.

2011

May 23, 2011
The 82nd Legislature passes Senate Bill 489, changing the designation of the Abilene, Breckenridge, and Brownwood Extension Centers and making them permanent locations. The name of the Abilene, Breckenridge, Brownwood, and Sweetwater locations is changed to a collective TSTC West Texas.

Summer 2011
TSTC Marshall opens the new "TNT Building," the Transportation and Technology Building, to house the industrial maintenance, diesel equipment, and welding technology programs.

August 2011
TSTC West Texas completes a multi-year, multi-million-dollar renovation of the Abilene campus, to include the conference room, library, learning lab, and student areas.

The Harlingen University Center.

Dedication of the Breckenridge Technology Center (top) and the interior of the renovated Brownwood Building 2 (bottom).

August 31, 2011
TSTC Harlingen dedicates the University Center, a multi-institution center with six universities offering forty-six bachelor's and master's degrees.

September 2011
TSTC West Texas dedicates the newest addition to the Breckenridge location, the Breckenridge Technology Center.

March 2012
TSTC West Texas's paramedic program earns national accreditation from the Commission on Accreditation of Allied Health Education Programs.

August 10, 2011
TSTC Waco and Temple College hold ribbon-cutting ceremonies at the temporary home of the East Williamson County Higher Education Center in Hutto at Veterans' Hill Elementary.

December 2011
TSTC West Texas completes $3.2 million in renovations to Brownwood Building 2.

The West Texas mobile training lab for welding (right) and its interior (above).

Texas State Technical College ™

Mobile Welding Instruction • Training at Your Location • 325-641-3921

2012

May 2012
TSTC West Texas receives funds from Jobs and Education for Texans, known as JET funds, to build a mobile training lab for welding, which will be used on-site at industrial and educational locations.

May 3, 2012
TSTC Waco holds a ribbon cutting for the 82,000-square-foot, state-of-the-art Colonel James T. Connally Aerospace Center.

May 16, 2012
The Marshall Chamber of Commerce and the Marshall Economic Development Corporation present TSTC Marshall with the Shining Star Award.

May 22, 2012
TSTC Waco holds a groundbreaking for the permanent location of the East Williamson County Higher Education Center in Hutto.

August 26, 2012
Classes begin at the temporary location for at the East Williamson County Higher Education Center.

August 30, 2012
TSTC West Texas hosts community leaders, automobile dealers, and State Representative Susan King at a demonstration of new alternative fuel simulators and training engines received through a $295,000 grant from the Texas Workforce Commission.

October 13, 2012
TSTC Waco holds grand-opening ceremonies for the East Williamson County Higher Education Center in Hutto at its temporary location.

2013
The magazine, *Military Times*, ranks TSTC number one in Texas and number eleven nationally in its "Best for Vets: Career and Technical Colleges 2013" article.

September 21, 2012
TSTC Harlingen opens a satellite location in Raymondville.

November 2012
TSTC Marshall encloses its outdoor pavilion to create the new 7,500-square-foot, multi-purpose Activity Center.

June 2013
TSTC Waco announces the approval of nearly $3 million in Texas Department of Transportation funding for airport runway and site upgrades.

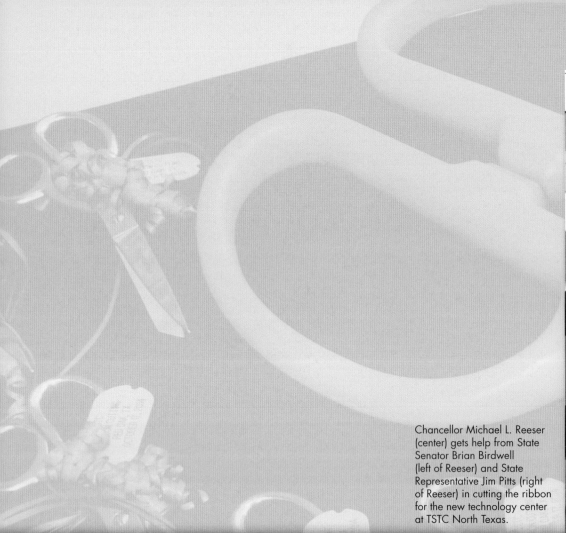

Chancellor Michael L. Reeser (center) gets help from State Senator Brian Birdwell (left of Reeser) and State Representative Jim Pitts (right of Reeser) in cutting the ribbon for the new technology center at TSTC North Texas.

2013

September 2013
The East Williamson County Higher Education Center opens for classes in a new building and its permanent location in Hutto.

September 1, 2013
TSTC Marshall opens a new extension center in Red Oak, TSTC North Texas.

November 2013
TSTC Waco and the Connally Independent School District submit an application for an Early College High School designation from the Texas Education Agency.

December 11, 2013
Administrators at the East Williamson County Higher Education Center sign a partnership agreement with Texas A&M University–Central Texas.

January 2014
TSTC Waco and the Connally Independent School District receive final approvals to open Connally Career Tech Early College High School for the 2014–2015 academic year.

January 13, 2014
TSTC North Texas begins holding classes.

January 13, 2014
Texas A&M University–Central Texas begins teaching classes at the East Williamson County Higher Education Center in Hutto.

August 14, 2014
The TSTC Board of Regents approves Minute Order 44-14(c) authorizing an expansion of TSTC's presence in Fort Bend County. Groundbreaking on a new campus location is expected in 2015 with an anticipated opening in 2016.

January 24, 2014
Texas House Appropriations Chairman Jim Pitts attends the groundbreaking ceremonies for the first building for TSTC North Texas in Red Oak.

October 17, 2014
TSTC North Texas holds dedication ceremonies for its first permanent building in Red Oak.

TSTC Students have more national SkillsUSA© medals than all other two-year and four-year Texas colleges combined.

Source Data: SkillsUSA©, 1980-2014

TSTC is #1 in Texas for conferring the most associate's degrees in engineering-related fields, computer & information science & support services, and precision production.

Source Data: Community College Week Top 100 Associate Degree Producers, 2014

We focus our efforts on just one thing:

helping students prepare for a great

career in a high-tech, high-demand

job. We don't believe that technical

education is about "getting in" to

college—it's about "getting out"

and into a job.

Kyle Smith
West Texas Interim President
Texas State Technical College

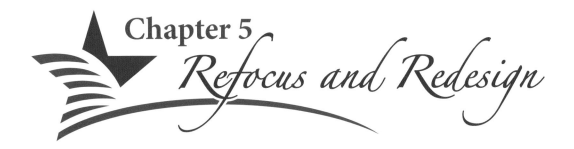

Chapter 5
Refocus and Redesign

Throughout the 1970s and 1980s, Texas State Technical Institute (TSTI) experienced continued growth and support from the legislature. Although only a few were successful, legislators made nearly a dozen attempts to create new TSTI campuses within their districts.

There was even an attempt in the mid-1980s to allow TSTI to award bachelor's degrees in technical fields. By the time TSTI's name changed to Texas State Technical College (TSTC) in 1991, TSTC consisted of campuses in Amarillo, Harlingen, Sweetwater, and Waco, as well as five extension centers located in Abilene, Breckenridge, Brownwood, Marshall, and McAllen.

TSTC's rapport within the legislature began to suffer by the mid-1990s, however. Manufacturing had declined throughout the 1980s, and the state's network of community colleges had grown. Enrollment on some campuses had also begun to decline. An internal document (author unknown) written just prior to the twenty-fifth anniversary alluded to the coming problems, "TSTI was born of necessity and early operated from a position of opportunity. More recently, it has taken a defensive posture trying to protect what it has rather than seeking to address the changed needs and concerns of potential students."

Many legislators sensed TSTC's apparent inability to adjust. They felt community colleges offered the same programs as TSTC and questioned the need for both college systems. As a result, TSTC administrators and community leaders representing individual campus locations had to fight off repeated attempts to restrict TSTC operations and/or to transfer campuses to community college districts. In the end, TSTC Amarillo and the McAllen Extension Center became the property of community colleges, but TSTC held on to all other locations.

The legislative battles meant morale was low at the campus level across the system. "People were worried about the survival of TSTC," said Dr. Bill Segura, who became TSTC's ninth chancellor in January of 1998. Segura's first task was to re-establish faith in the TSTC brand. He did that by addressing the internal morale concerns through stakeholder visioning meetings and by rebuilding relationships within the legislature and with community colleges. He also established an External Relations Office in Austin so TSTC could be more responsive to legislative concerns. According to Segura, "Connections are important when fixing a tarnished brand or when creating a new one." The primary role of TSTC's External Relations Office was to establish those connections with the legislative offices and to ensure communication channels remained open. Rebuilding the TSTC brand was a slow process and took several legislative sessions.

Dr. Bill Segura, Chancellor, 1998–2010

By 2007, legislative leaders wanted more accountability in state spending and began a push for outcomes-based funding for higher education. Although most institutions were skeptical about the

concept, Segura embraced it. "I have always believed in outcomes-based funding. I was drawn to the model because of the leavers." According to Segura, higher education has traditionally treated all leavers the same. The measure has always been the degree earned, not the job gained. Many technical students leave prior to graduation because they have mastered the training needed for the job they wanted. In an outcomes-based funding model, that constitutes a success.

Accordingly, an outcomes-based model is peculiarly suited for technical education because the focus of technical education is jobs. Skills determine success in a job, and skills mastery does not always require a full degree program. Calling it a "success-only model," Segura quickly saw its potential for TSTC. "I believe it is the future of technical education." It affords more program flexibility for the institution and reduces training time for students, allowing them to enter the workforce faster.

The transition from one funding model to another did not come easily. "That kind of dramatic change is really difficult to bring about," said Segura. TSTC's leadership, though, accepted the

2007
The 80th Legislature asks Texas State Technical College (TSTC) and other institutions to consider outcomes-based funding. TSTC Chancellor Bill Segura responds favorably.

2009
The 81st Legislature, under Rider 52 of the Appropriations Bill, directs TSTC, the Texas Higher Education Coordinating Board, the Texas Workforce Commission, and the Texas Comptroller's Office to determine the feasibility of an outcomes-based funding model for TSTC.

2008
TSTC commissions an independent study to design and validate a preliminary funding model based upon the economic impact of graduates and their earnings, instead of teaching activities or the number of contact hours.

2010
The Texas Higher Education Coordinating Board commissions an outside consultant to conduct the feasibility study and concludes that an outcomes-based funding model has merit for TSTC.

2007

The New Funding Formula

challenge and embarked upon a systemic overhaul by restructuring program offerings and developing new methods of instructional delivery. "A success-only model, which funds our work based only upon outcomes, meant our internal focus had to shift from processes to the students and the industries that employ them. The only way we could succeed as instructors and as an institution was to ensure that our students succeeded in the marketplace."

For the next six years and three legislative sessions, TSTC worked with the legislature and state agencies to validate the concept. Finally, in 2013, the legislature made TSTC the first college in America whose funding is based solely upon student employment outcomes. The funding method, now known as the "value-added" or "returned-value" funding model, uses actual state tax revenues attributable to student earnings after leaving TSTC as the basis for paying TSTC. It means TSTC gets paid only after the student gets a job and begins paying taxes. The model fits TSTC's statewide mission to "improve the competitiveness of Texas business and industry" and, for the first time, rewards successful student employment, rather than enrollment.

Segura believes TSTC is one of only a few institutions in the nation that could have accomplished such a dramatic transition. "Today, the patina on the TSTC brand is shiny and strong. It always has been with industry." Segura says technical education, in particular, must move quickly to refocus on jobs and student success. "It is no longer about playing school; it is about learning how to work." At TSTC, students learn skills, and they get great jobs. That is success.

2011
The 82nd Legislature, under Rider 42 of the Appropriations Bill, directs TSTC, the Texas Higher Education Coordinating Board, the Texas Workforce Commission, and the Comptroller's Office to develop a funding formula for TSTC based upon the imputed economic value of the earnings of TSTC students once they enter the Texas workforce.

2012
TSTC and the agencies, joined by the Legislative Budget Board and the Ray Marshall Center at the University of Texas, develop the first version of an outcomes-based funding model for TSTC. The Texas Higher Education Coordinating Board and the TSTC Board of Regents approve the funding methodology.

2013
The 83rd Legislature, under Rider 11, adopts a "value-added" or "returned-value" funding model for all TSTC campuses affecting the 2014–2015 biennial appropriations. The legislature also directs the relevant agencies to refine the funding formula prior to the next budget cycle in order to further "the goal of rewarding job placement and graduate earnings projections, not time in training or contact hours."

The Cake Pop Briefing

The External Relations Office began the process of educating staff at the Texas State Capitol about the proposed "value-added" funding model before the 2013 legislative session even began. One such effort was to host a briefing, which included an informative presentation by Chancellor Michael L. Reeser, as well as a hands-on cooking demonstration by Waco's culinary team—complete with aprons, chef hats, and takeaways for participants. This briefing became known as the "Cake Pop Briefing" and was successful in helping legislative staff understand the nuances of the new funding plan. After seven years of work, the 83rd Legislature finally adopted the new funding method for Texas State Technical College before adjourning sine die in May 2013.

Chef Mark Schneider

Mark Schneider
Culinary Arts Department Chair
TSTC Waco

Chef Mark Schneider is the 2013–2015 president of the Texas Chefs Association and holds several certifications from the American Culinary Federation. In 2008, the American Academy of Chefs named him Texas Chef of the Year. Even with such an impressive résumé, Schneider is most proud of his role in designing what he terms "the gem of the campus"—the new Greta W. Watson Culinary Arts Center on the Waco campus.

"The great thing about all of the culinary arts programs at Texas State Technical College is that the total cost for a certificate or two-year degree is a third or less of the cost for comparable training at similar schools in Texas," Schneider said. "I met a chef recently who graduated from a culinary program in Dallas ten years ago, and he's still paying back his student loans. A high percentage of our students have jobs when they graduate. They leave here with top-grade skills they can take anywhere in the world and succeed."

TSTC Day at the Texas Capitol

In an effort to build the brand and name recognition for Texas State Technical College (TSTC) within the legislature, the External Relations Office hosts TSTC Day at the Capitol during each legislative session. The day's festivities include recognition by the House and Senate, interactive program displays from the campuses, and a small gift for each legislative office delivered by TSTC student ambassadors. During recent sessions, administrators and members of the TSTC Board of Regents have also hosted an afternoon ice cream social for legislators and their staff.

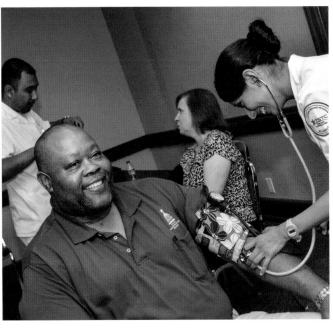

Ron Widup

A 1982 Waco graduate in electrical power technology, Ron Widup boasts a career of more than thirty-one years at Shermco Industries. There, he has risen from a field service technician to president and chief executive officer of the international company, which focuses on the testing, repair, maintenance, and analysis of power distribution systems.

To those trying to decide upon an education and career path, Widup says, "There is no doubt this is a great time to be in a technical field. Invest a little time and a little money, and come out with a great career. Demand is great so you can immediately get a great paying job without bankrupting the start of your life."

Widup stays involved with Texas State Technical College (TSTC), serving on advisory committees and helping to develop curriculum. Shermco has also donated an electronics lab on the Waco campus. He challenges other industry leaders to do the same. "Get involved. If you want to differentiate your product and make yourself different from the other guy, what better way than to start at the foundational level with the technical schools? Let them know what you need, and TSTC will produce graduates ready to go to work."

Ron Widup, president and chief executive officer of Shermco Industries, inspires a group of student ambassadors at the 2013 TSTC Day at the Capitol, as he describes the journey which led him to the head office of an international company after graduating from Texas State Technical College with a two-year degree.

MR. CARR
PEC Safety

In a continuing effort to strengthen relationships with state and congressional leaders, Colonel Randall Wooten (Retired), then president of the Marshall campus of Texas State Technical College, testifies about the college's programs for veterans at an oversight hearing for the Subcommittee on Economic Opportunity, part of the House Committee on Veterans' Affairs. The hearing was held in Washington, DC, on May 20, 2014. Colonel Wooten now serves as vice chancellor and chief execution officer for TSTC. (Photo by Ian Wagreich Photography)

COL. WOOTEN (USAF, Ret.)
Texas State Technical College in Marshall

MR. EVERE
Center for Employment Tra

Our economy is suffering from a

shortage of technically trained workers.

That is why demand for TSTC's training

will increase in the years to come and

why it's vitally important for TSTC to stay

ahead of the game.

Michael L. Reeser
Chancellor
Texas State Technical College

Chapter 6
Vision, a Portal to the Future

Less than two decades ago, most anyone traveling in the eastern part of Williamson County, just north of Austin, would have seen rows and rows of crops in agricultural production. When the Avery's looked out over their family's heritage farm, however, they saw something very different.

They saw a cluster of educational and medical facilities intended to serve one of the fastest growing regions in the nation. By 2013, the Avery vision for their ancestors' homestead was a reality and included Texas State Technical College (TSTC) at the East Williamson County Higher Education Center in Hutto.

The Avery family vision is just one of many dreams woven into the fabric of TSTC's fifty-year history, a history nurtured by strong leaders and enhanced by the dreams and visions of many who dared to believe in them. For the student, the dream may have been a future different from his family's experience as migrant workers. For the instructor, the dream may have been a chance to teach and direct the course of an emerging industry in Texas. For the community, the dream may have been an educational facility intended to bolster a sagging economy. The dreams and visions varied, but they all required someone to take a first step in order to make them a reality.

According to TSTC Regent John Henry "Jack" Kultgen, Governor John B. Connally's original vision for TSTC included more than a single campus. He wanted a chain of technical schools across Texas. Today, TSTC consists of eleven campus locations, as well as numerous partnerships with public school districts and other institutions of higher education. The campuses in Hutto, Red Oak, and Fort Bend County have been added only within the last two years, and demand for additional locations is growing. Governor Connally's vision, although birthed more than a half-century ago, is still evolving.

TSTC's legislatively mandated statewide mission is to "facilitate and deliver an articulated and responsive technical education system." With the growing shortage of skilled workers, the word "responsive" is keenly relevant to Chancellor Michael L. Reeser who believes education is in the midst of a massive culture shift driven by technology. "In the years ahead, TSTC must move away

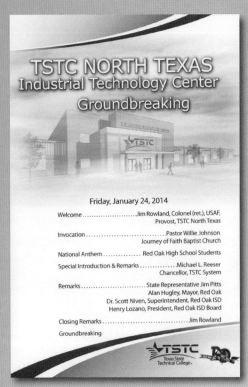

TSTC NORTH TEXAS
Industrial Technology Center
Groundbreaking

Friday, January 24, 2014

Welcome.............................Jim Rowland, Colonel (ret.), USAF,
Provost, TSTC North Texas

Invocation..Pastor Willie Johnson
Journey of Faith Baptist Church

National Anthem...............Red Oak High School Students

Special Introduction & Remarks...............Michael L. Reeser
Chancellor, TSTC System

Remarks...........................State Representative Jim Pitts
Alan Hugley, Mayor, Red Oak
Dr. Scott Niven, Superintendent, Red Oak ISD
Henry Lozano, President, Red Oak ISD Board

Closing Remarks...Jim Rowland

Groundbreaking

TSTC
Texas State
Technical College.

A Big Deal

At the January 24, 2014, groundbreaking for the North Texas campus of Texas State Technical College (TSTC), Red Oak Mayor Alan Hugley related a local high school student's excitement about the new TSTC campus. The student planned to study heating and air conditioning maintenance (HVAC) at TSTC and pictured a time in the future when the temperature would be over one hundred degrees outside and the air conditioning would break down. Hugley told the North Texas audience the student acknowledged that others could get fancier degrees; but, as an HVAC technician on a hot day, he was going to be as important as anyone.

Hugley said of the new campus, "This is a big deal. There is nothing more important than a new generation of young people who have a chance to change their futures and change their lives."

Current Board of Regents Chairman Ellis M. Skinner II and past Board of Regents Chairman Dr. Rolf R. Haberecht at the groundbreaking for the North Texas Industrial Technology Center.

THE MARSHALL
NEWS MESSENGER
MarshallNewsMessenger.com

MARSHALL, TEXAS   WEDNESDAY, JUNE 6, 2012   50 CENTS

TSTC first college in nation to fund by results

Official: Current model has 'no accountability'

By HANNAH DECLERK
HDECLERK@MARSHALLNEWSMESSENGER.COM

Texas State Technical College is the first college in the nation whose instructional funding will be determined solely by results or outcomes.

The "Returned Value" funding model is collaboration be-tween the Texas High Education Coordinating Board, TSTC and the Legislative Budget Board, and other relevant agencies.

The funding formula will be implemented for the 2014-15 biennium, and will reward job placement and graduate earn-ings projections instead of time training or contract hours.

"Right now every public education institution in Texas is paid on some sort of contact hour formula, which is basically how long you keep a student in a seat per semester," TSTC-Marshall President Randall Wooten said. "But the problem with contact hour funding, there is no accountability."

According to Wooten, TSTC officials began corresponding with legislatures about five years ago about having a portion of their pay for perfor-mance.

He said performance can be defined by a lot of different metrics and each place a per-formance can look different for different institutions.

"People come here for skills. And we call that placement. placing someone in a job or ca-reer. That is a metric we want to be measured by and the state legislature has accepted that," he said.

Currently, the college has a job placement rate at nearly 90 percent.

"The formula works very

note the formula works well with TSTC because the institu-tion's overall focus is to place students in jobs as quickly as possible.

See Funding, Page 3A

from a product-centric model which uses inflexible curriculum and inflexible schedules. Instead, we must build customized educational pathways for each major industrial workforce need. Additionally, we must adjust these pathways to account for a student's previous education or work experience."

Reeser points to history to explain his meaning. The Industrial Revolution led the way to mass production of goods and a "one-size-fits-all" way of doing things. "Today's educational process is an allegory for the assembly-line style of production in which students are moved along in a highly standardized fashion." Reeser believes today's technology, however, can restore the ability to practice "mass customization," even in education. He foresees TSTC students following an individualized pathway through technical curriculum, one that is customized to the student's learning pace and to his targeted career.

Reeser sees the legislature's adoption of TSTC's new value-added funding model as essential to the institution's ability to fulfill its mission for Texas and to meet the imperative for customized training. "In order for institutions like TSTC to implement these new educational models, it

Chancellor Michael L. Reeser's motto

is necessary for the state to employ a new way of paying for them. In particular, funding must be driven by results, not process."

Because demand for skills education is growing exponentially, Reeser contends that TSTC must be both deliberate and nimble about finding new ways to get things done. He points to TSTC's competency-based approach to learning as one example. This learning model disconnects learning from a calendar-driven process and, instead, allows the student's ability to master the material to drive the pace. Transportable micro-credentials, which are readily accepted by industry, are another of Reeser's examples.

By transitioning to such innovative educational approaches, Reeser believes TSTC will help its students move into the workforce faster. "These new approaches will improve student outcomes while reducing costs all around—for students, for the institution, and for the state. It is a more efficient way to train Texas' workforce."

Reeser sees the need for innovation as urgent. "Our economy is suffering from a shortage of technically trained workers. That is why demand for TSTC's training will increase in the years to come and why it's vitally important for TSTC to stay ahead of the game."

The chancellor is passionate about what he sees as the future for TSTC. It is a vision not so different from Governor Connally's original dream for James Connally Technical Institute. Two visions, two leaders, one goal— to make TSTC "the most sophisticated technical vocational training institute in the country." In 2015, Texas State Technical College remains uniquely positioned to turn vision into reality.

BRECKENRIDGE
MARSHALL
RED OAK
ABILENE
SWEETWATER
BROWNWOOD
WACO
HUTTO
FORT BEND
INGLESIDE
HARLINGEN

Four to One

Texas State Technical College (TSTC) currently has eleven locations across Texas and has received requests for more. Texas deserves a responsive system of technical education to meet its workforce needs; however, TSTC's historical structure of four separately accredited colleges can complicate the process of bringing new locations on line. TSTC has never been shy about employing innovation, so the solution is a bold, but beneficial one.

As this work goes to press, TSTC has launched the process that will consolidate the four colleges into a single statewide institution. This reorganization will reduce unnecessary duplication of efforts, optimize the organization for expansion, and—most importantly—concentrate more resources on educating students. This new unified structure will provide TSTC with the right internal organization to meet the challenges of the next fifty years.

Pictured left to right are Dr. Glenda O. Barron, president of Temple College; Christina Avery Fell; Dr. A. Nelson Avery; John S. Avery Sr.; Charles N. Avery III; and Dr. Elton E. Stuckly Jr., currently vice chancellor and chief operations officer for Texas State Technical College.

EAST WILLIAMSON COUNTY
HIGHER EDUCATION CENTER - HUT...

The Avery Family

The Avery family's history in Williamson County dates back to 1854 when Arvid and Anna Lena Nelson arrived in northeast Round Rock from Barkeryd Parish, Jonkoping, Sweden, with their four children. The Nelsons were an industrious family of farmers and merchants. By 1900, they had amassed a large block of farmland within the county and numerous businesses in downtown Round Rock.

The Nelson patriarchs and their descendants devoted themselves to building churches and educational institutions while growing their community. In 1905, the Avery family joined the Nelson family with the marriage of Charles N. Avery Sr. and Adla Nelson. The following years demonstrated that the Avery offspring adhered to the Nelson's priority upon public service.

Members of the Avery family of today are fifth generation descendants of Arvid and Anna Lena Nelson. They include siblings Charles N. Avery III, John S. Avery, Dr. A. Nelson Avery, and Christina Avery Fell.

In 2005, the Avery siblings began developing Avery Farms, a portion of the original Nelson Estate established prior to 1900. The development plan for Avery Farms was to create an education and medically oriented, mixed-use development in northeast Round Rock. The development is now home to the Seton Williamson Hospital, as well as to new campuses for Texas State University, Austin Community College, and the Texas A&M Health Science Center College of Medicine—all beneficiaries of donated Avery land.

The multi-institution teaching center in Hutto, just a few miles from the Round Rock mixed-use development, is also a beneficiary of the Avery family's generosity. Opening in the fall of 2013, the East Williamson County Higher Education Center houses Temple College, Texas A&M University Central Texas, and Texas State Technical College (TSTC).

Acknowledging that many might think the idea to be "hokey," Charles Avery said, "We believe we have a stewardship regarding that property." He added the siblings have purposefully sought to find its highest and best use. They believe they have now done that.

With the addition of TSTC's technical program offerings, the collection of higher education institutions now located on the old Nelson homestead represents a sampling of all higher education has to offer. It is a sampling which Charles Avery tasted personally. Despite an accomplished background in banking and commercial construction, he enrolled in the first welding class TSTC ever offered at the Hutto facility.

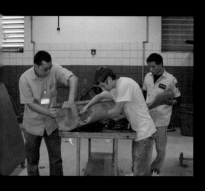

PROJECT MUSTANG

The 50th Anniversary Committee wanted to have a system project that would showcase the work and talents of students and would become emblematic of the anniversary celebration. From the committee's visioning sessions, Project Mustang was born. A 1965 Mustang convertible was located and purchased. Students from Harlingen, Waco, and West Texas then spent a year refurbishing the vehicle. Campuses and student organizations will use Project Mustang for parades and special events as a symbol of Texas State Technical College's fifty-year legacy.

STUDENTS WHO WORKED ON PROJECT MUSTANG:

Bruce Luna	Juan Vences	Michael Reyes
Cody Clark	Trio Jimenez	Noe Cardona
Justin Owen	David Taber	Chris Ratliff
Paul Robinson	Philip McKee	Dylan Edwards
Steven Larrabee	Keith Soto	Tyler Lassiter
Kegan Schmidt	Christopher Denson	Angel Sorola
Anthony Taylor	Jordan Eppler	Ivis Torres
Raul Lopez	Jesus Benitez	Erasmo Parra
Luiz Loredo	Derek Schilhab	Roberto Rodriguez
Alexa Shed	Joe Keggler	Ricardo Benavidez
Corey Zavala		

INSTRUCTORS WHO WORKED ON PROJECT MUSTANG:

Clint Campbell – Project Leader
Ranson Bandy
Kevon Kleibrink
Max Fowler
Tracy Marshall
Jacob Pevia
Jerome Carter – Retired
Jose Vargas
Rodney Rivera
Jeffery Looper – Director Transportation and Service Division

TSTC

Members of the board of regents pose with Chancellor Michael L. Reeser and Project Mustang. Pictured left to right are Keith Honey, Linda McKenna, J. V. Martin, Chancellor Reeser, Joe Hearne, Ivan Andarza, John Hatchel, Penny Forrest, Chairman Ellis M. Skinner II, and Joe Gurecky.

Like most evolving technologies, those related to electrical power generation, distribution, and controls are changing almost every day. That means we must meet the challenge to keep up with these changes and make sure our graduates are equipped to hit the ground running the minute they graduate.

Like a lot of the older programs, our success is built upon a wonderful history and legacy. I'm a graduate of Texas State Technical College, and my oldest boy is in the electrical power and controls program right now.

Mike Bowers Sr.
Instructor and Department Chair
Electrical Power and Controls Program
Texas State Technical College Waco

Chapter 7
Training a Workforce

Texas State Technical College (TSTC) is different than other state educational institutions, and it is different on purpose. The distinction begins with TSTC's statutory mission.

Although TSTC is a two-year educational institution, unlike other two-year schools, its mission is statewide and includes a focus in both technical-vocational education and economic development. In short, TSTC is charged with growing the state's economic competiveness by ensuring the Texas workforce has the right skills at the right time, especially in advanced and emerging technologies.

TSTC's dual role in technical education and economic development means programs constantly evolve to meet industry needs. It also means they are specific to regional needs. For example, Harlingen's agricultural technology program is not offered at TSTC North Texas in Red Oak. In order to ensure skills match industry needs, curriculum is guided by program-specific advisory committees consisting of ten to thirty industry experts. Advisory committees meet several times a year to fine-tune program outcomes and ensure graduates are job-ready.

Because of the focus on current technology and existing market needs, programs may cycle in and out of TSTC's course catalog. Building construction technology is an example of a program area that was popular early in TSTC's history, then cycled out and has now returned. Although periodically evolving to match current technologies, other programs have always been part of the TSTC curricula. Examples include welding, electrical and electronics technologies, automotive technology and collision repair, and health science technologies.

Although some once-popular programs are now absent from current course guides, they do offer an interesting "throw-back" to life in the 1960s, 1970s, and 1980s. These include livestock and ranch operations, agricultural seed quality and processing, meat processing, aquaculture (fish farming), supermarket management, leather processing, and jukebox and pinball machine service and repair.

These obsolete programs also speak to TSTC's focus on training workers for existing jobs. If there are no longer jobs in a particular program area, the program is removed from TSTC's course offerings. TSTC's connection to industry allows campuses to be responsive to fluctuations in market demand and industry needs. In fact, harkening back to TSTC's mission of economic development, the legislature has specifically directed TSTC to be the state's forecaster of emerging technologies in order to anticipate and develop necessary new technical education program areas.

TSTC's eye to the future has led to many cutting-edge programs, including nanotechnology, wind and solar energy, fuel cells, laser electro-optics, digital forensics, robotics, and game and simulation programming. The resolve to anticipate and respond to the needs of the state's dynamic economy remains the primary focus of TSTC's partnerships with employers, local governments, other educational institutions, and the Texas Legislature. Today, TSTC awards associate's degrees and certificates in more than two hundred different programs and specializations on its various campuses.

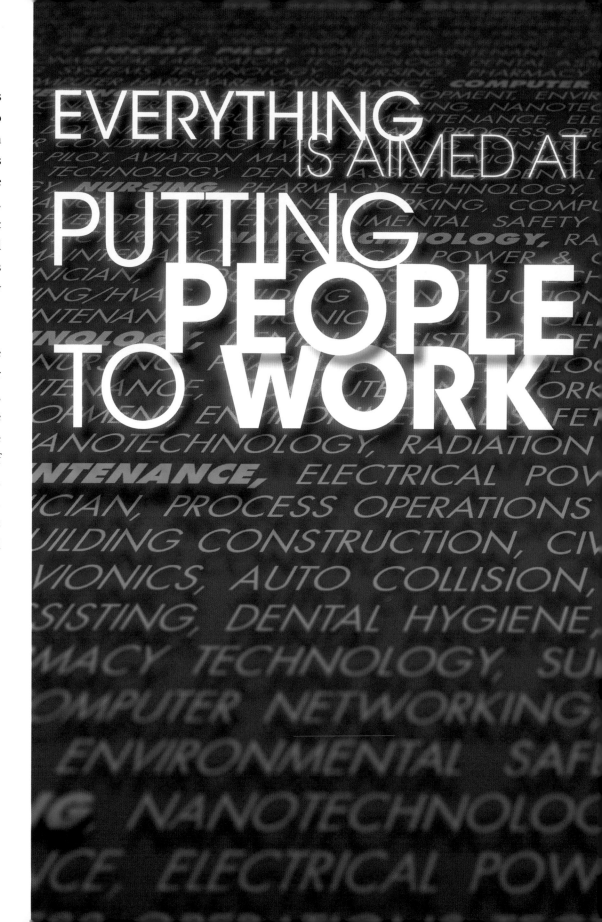

EVERYTHING IS AIMED AT PUTTING PEOPLE TO WORK

Texas State Technical College offers a wide array of technical programs involving agriculture, hospitality, architecture, construction, transportation, health sciences, information technology, energy, and manufacturing. The program offerings at each campus are unique and specifically designed to meet local workforce needs. Together, they represent **124 associate's degree programs** and **133 certificate programs** (as of December 2014).

Texas State Technical College's portfolio of programs is continuously evolving to meet industry demand. For the most up-to-date listing of program offerings, see a current course catalog. Note not all programs are offered at every TSTC location.

http://www.tstc.edu/careerprograms/careers

Bob Lovelace

Department Chair, Master Instructor
Instrumentation, Computerized Controls & Robotics
TSTC Waco

Bob Lovelace is a 1983 graduate of Texas State Technical Institute. Today, he is the department chair of the instrumentation, computerized controls, and robotics program at the Waco campus of Texas State Technical College (TSTC). He is a master instructor in the program his father, Richard Carl Lovelace, designed.

Lovelace, who returned to TSTC as an instructor after a decade in industry, says he has stayed because he likes building success stories. "Students are my product. My job is to build the best and most job-ready entry-level technicians I can. Everything I do is aimed at one goal—putting people to work."

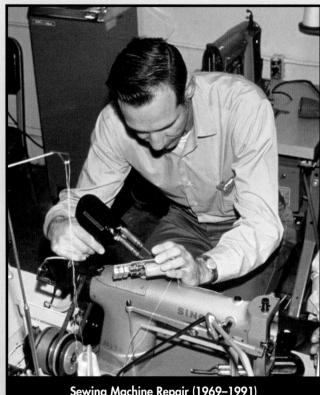

Sewing Machine Repair (1969–1991)

Floriculture and Ornamental Horticulture Technology, Floral Design (1967–1991)

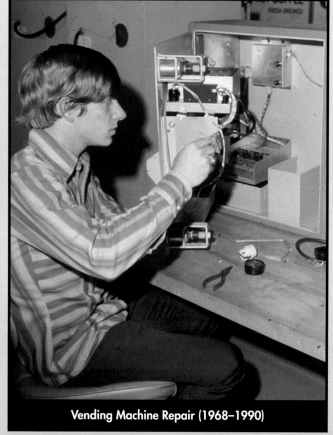

Vending Machine Repair (1968–1990)

Radio and Television Servicing (1968–1996)

Seed and Grain Technology (1971–1991)

Animal/Veterinary Technology (1971–1991)

Texas State Technical College

Supermarket Management (1977–1991)

Scientific Data Processing (1967–1969)

Audio Visual Production Technology (1970–1999)

Games Specialist and Automatic Phonographs (1969-1970)

Underwater Welding (1971–1983)

Greta W. Watson
Culinary Arts Center

(Photo by Marlene S. McMichael)

Culinary

Glen Bedgood
Director of Industrial Training
TSTC West Texas

Glen Bedgood came to Texas State Technical College (TSTC) as a computer science instructor in 1981 when the college was still called Texas State Technical Institute. He eventually became dean of instruction at the Sweetwater campus. With the introduction of the wind energy and turbine technology program, however, Bedgood's lifelong interests in rock climbing and rappelling became part of his professional qualifications.

Training in safety and rescue became a necessary part of the curriculum when TSTC purchased a wind turbine for instructional purposes. Rather than sending students elsewhere for the specialization, Bedgood and his colleagues obtained certifications as rescue technicians and then as rescue instructors. "I didn't know what to expect when I started at TSTC," Bedgood laughs. "I figured I would only be here for two or three years, but I've loved my duties at TSTC. I enjoy the experience of changing students' lives for the better, and it is gratifying to learn that one of our graduates rescued a fellow worker from a life-threatening situation."

Glen Bedgood, Director of Industrial Training, Sweetwater campus (Courtesy of Glenn Bedgood)

Programs That *Are*

Wind Energy and Turbine Technology

Electrical Power—Line Technician

Solar Energy Technology

Glen Bedgood's view from the top of a wind turbine (Courtesy of Glen Bedgood)

Energy Production and Management

James Allen

Dissatisfied with his career in health care finance, James Allen decided to switch gears and enroll in the process operations technology program at Texas State Technical College (TSTC) in Marshall. "The program opened my eyes to the way you actually apply scientific principles. I couldn't have asked for a better foundation." Allen finished the program in 2007 and is now the production team lead at a Texas Chevron facility.

Prior to his current position, Allen was Chevron's operations and maintenance recruiter, hiring graduates from two-year schools like TSTC. He believes industry should have a symbiotic relationship with technical schools, providing technical expertise and financial backing to ensure quality, work-ready graduates. As a result, Allen serves as chairman of TSTC Marshall's advisory committee for the instrumentation and process operations programs. "You can't beat the real-world aspect of the instruction at any of the TSTC campuses. If an individual is willing to grab the opportunity, TSTC will provide an avenue for an individual to move forward with a great career."

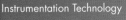
Instrumentation Technology

Downhole Tool Technology (Photo by Marlene S. McMichael)

Electrical Power and Control Technology

Wind Energy and Turbine Technology

Jean A. Lashbrook, RN
Instructor and Director Nursing
TSTC Harlingen

"For years, there have been rumors that changes in health care costs and delivery would negatively impact the nursing and medical support industries. The reason that's not likely to happen is that hospitals, clinics, and doctors' offices will always require the basic skills and services of medical assistants, nurses, emergency medical technicians, and dental assistants. If anything, graduates of Texas State Technical College's allied health programs will be in even more demand over the next few decades."

Programs That Are

Pharmacy Technician

Dental Assistant

Surgical Technology

Emergency Medical Technology

Nursing

Health Sciences

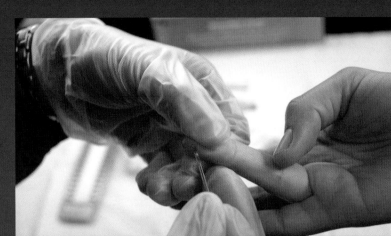
Dental Laboratory Technology

Nursing

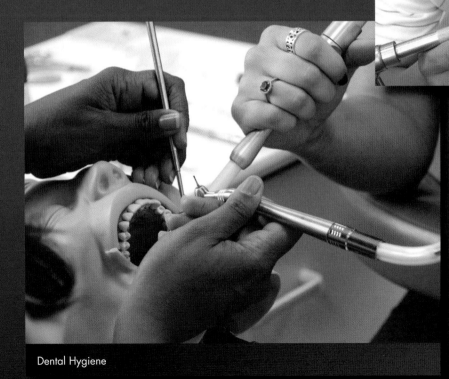
Dental Hygiene

Nursing

Samantha Clark

Despite going into labor during semester exams, Samantha Clark has nothing but positive remarks about the nursing program at Texas State Technical College (TSTC) in West Texas. "The program chair is a NICU [neonatal intensive care] nurse, so I knew we were covered." Clark, a 2012 honors graduate from the nursing program, also earned the distinguished President's Award. "TSTC instructors are amazing. They desire to see you succeed and pass your nursing board exams on the first try. I always recommend TSTC." The nursing program at TSTC West Texas achieved a 100 percent pass rate in its 2012 state-administered exit exams. Clark is a nurse at Abilene Regional Medical Center and is pursuing a bachelor's degree in nursing.

Robb McMahan

Robb McMahan enrolled in what is now called software development technology at Texas State Technical College (TSTC) in Marshall during a hiatus from his award-winning career as a recording artist. He had grown weary of performing on the road, so McMahan was intent upon trying out his second love, computers. The year was 2007; and, by mid-year, Steve Jobs would introduce his first iPhone. "I became enamored with the technology. I had to learn how to do that."

While learning the basic building blocks and root languages at TSTC, McMahan traveled across the country to attend weekend boot camps to learn iPhone gaming and how to build mobile applications or "apps." McMahan released his first gaming app for the iPhone while still at TSTC and never looked back. "I have no regrets. I am known as a geek person now—a cool rock guitar player turned geeky nerd." McMahan now lives in California and works with DIRECTV creating apps for Apple products.

Robb McMahan accepts his degree from President Randall Wooten. (Courtesy of Robb McMahan)

Robb McMahan enjoying his success. (Courtesy of Robb McMahan)

Programs That *Are*

Game and Interactive Media Design

Digital Forensics Technology

High Performance Computing Technology

Computer Maintenance Technology

Information Technology

Visual Communications

Visual Communications and Design Digital Photography

Web Design and Development

Computer Science Technology

High Performance Computing

Jeff Horn

Standing in front of Baylor University's massive, new football stadium, Jeff Horn found himself back in Waco, but not as a student. This time, he was in Waco as the head construction manager for the new Baylor stadium. Horn earned a degree in building construction (BCT) in 1985 on the Waco campus and has risen from field engineer to senior superintendent in his twenty-nine years at Austin Commercial, an Austin Industries Company and one of the nation's largest and most diversified commercial builders.

Horn's introduction to Texas State Technical Institute came from Jay Tribble of Tribble & Stephens Construction Ltd. Tribble was a member of Waco's advisory committee for BCT from 1983 through 1990.

The BCT program was discontinued in 1991, but returned to the Texas State Technical College (TSTC) curriculum in 2007. Horn is glad to see it back. "Teaching an actual skill is something lacking in most educational programs today," says Horn. "Having the education from a college like TSTC can give you an advantage in the marketplace and on the actual job. By doing the hands-on training and getting out of school early, I was ahead of my friends who went to four-year schools. I was 20 when I started at Austin Commercial."

Land Surveying Technology

Drafting and Design Technology

Building Construction Trades Technology

Jeff Horn was the head construction manager for the new home of the Baylor Bears, McLane Stadium in Waco, Texas.

Building Construction Trades Technology

Plumbing and Pipefitting

Architecture, Construction, and Trades

Building Construction Trades Technology

Welding Technology

Building Construction Trades Technology

Building Construction Trades Technology

Air Conditioning and Refrigeration Technology

Drafting and Design Technology

Welding Technology

Edward Chaney
Industrial Maintenance Instructor
TSTC Marshall

Like many of the Texas State Technical College (TSTC) faculty, Edward Chaney's career began in the military. Building on his experience as a journeyman electrical equipment repairman in the US Marine Corps, Chaney worked as a private industry electrician, earning two degrees at TSTC along the way. He returned to TSTC as an instructor excited about the career outlook for his industrial maintenance students.

"Our program graduates are in heavy demand by all kinds of employers in the Marshall area," he said. "We not only give our people the multi-craft skills to maintain or repair just about any kind of system, but we impress upon them the need to be adaptable and to keep learning and expanding their capabilities as technologies change."

Chaney is just as enthusiastic about TSTC's role in the economy and future of Texas. "TSTC graduates keep Texas running. Our graduates make a real difference—saving their employers money by repairing, recycling, and keeping things operating at maximum efficiency."

Programs That *Are*

Industrial Systems Engineering Technology

Chemical/Environmental Technology

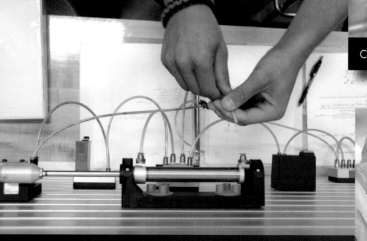

Laser/Electro Optics Technology

Nanotechnology

Manufacturing

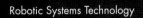
Robotic Systems Technology

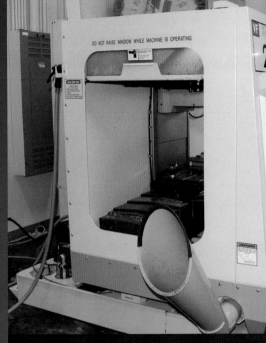

Mechanical Engineering Technology

Environmental Compliance Technology

Mechanical Engineering Technology

Laser/Electro Optics Technology

Aircraft Dispatch Technology

Air Traffic Control

Helicopter Pilot Training

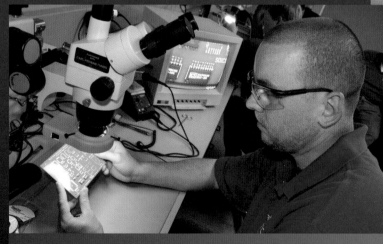

Avionics Technology

Aircraft Pilot Training

Transportation

Automotive Technology

Auto Collision and Management Technology

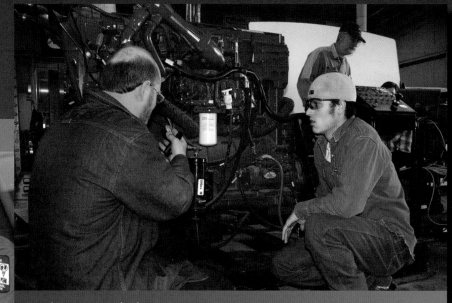

Diesel Equipment Technology

Diesel Equipment Technology

Colonel James T. Connally Aerospace Center

The primary goal of education, I

think, should be to enable people to

live effectively at [the] limits of their

abilities. Our challenge is to educate for

a living, as well as for making a living.

Governor Preston Smith
Opening remarks at
Texas Technical Society
October 1970

Chapter 8
Changed Lives

Texas State Technical College (TSTC) is founded upon the belief that, with marketable skills, people can access meaningful work and can, thereby, pursue their goals as responsible citizens.

Students often leave TSTC and remain successful in the same field throughout their careers. For others, TSTC reveals a pathway to higher education not previously thought possible. In either case, a life is changed and a brighter future is created.

TSTC's history is replete with success stories from former students. Examples include the non-traditional students, like Wallace Luna who lost his job and came to TSTC for re-training with a family in tow. Nearly twenty years later, Luna is the senior networking coordinator with the Texas Farm Bureau. TSTC's history also includes young men fresh out of the military, like Dan Garza who entered the workforce immediately out of TSTC and continued his education in order to earn a managerial position with 3M. It includes low-income students and frequent trouble makers, like Gregoria Arellano Jr. who discovered through TSTC's hands-on learning model that he could actually learn and turned that discovery into a career as an elementary

school principal. Too, TSTC's history includes individuals with award-winning careers, like Robb McMahan who decided to change course, pursue another passion, and ended up creating another success story with the skills he learned at TSTC.

Because TSTC's focus is on building Texas's workforce and teaching in-demand skills, an education at TSTC translates into a job. A job translates into a future. That is because many of TSTC's programs result in starting salaries above what is available to entry-level candidates with bachelor's degrees.

Perhaps Governor Preston Smith said it best in his opening remarks at a conference for the Texas Technical Society nearly forty-five years ago.

> The primary goal of education, I think, should be to enable people to live effectively at [the] limits of their abilities. Our challenge is to educate for a living, as well as for making a

Growing Leadership

For a statewide college system to innovate, collaborate, and be responsive to the workforce needs of Texas, it needs strong, effective leaders at all levels of the organization. For that reason, Texas State Technical College (TSTC) created a new program in 2010 to invest in the leadership development of its faculty and staff. In its first five years, the TSTC Leadership Institute has guided more than eighty employees through a rigorous yearlong leadership challenge, in which they learn to develop their passion for TSTC, build their confidence, and grow their leadership skills.

living. All the parts and all the efforts of both must be equally valued and respected. We have too long encouraged separatism in education through special programs and special emphasis for this and that.

…If we want to erase the physical scars of slums, poverty and crime and the mental scars of broken homes and wasted humanity, we must place a higher value on technical-vocational training. (*Texas Technical Society Journal,* October 1970)

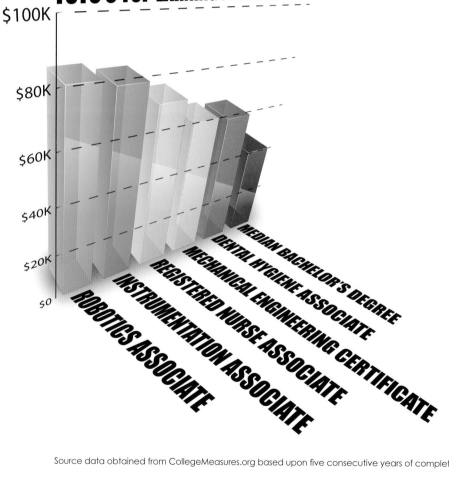

Source data obtained from CollegeMeasures.org based upon five consecutive years of completer outcomes.

Albert Chronis

Albert Chronis, a 2000 Harlingen graduate in computer-aided drafting and design, used his technical training to support himself while pursuing a degree in architecture. "My degree from Texas State Technical College [TSTC] opened my eyes to different opportunities and to what else I could do." Chronis is now a project manager for SpawGlass in the Rio Grande Valley and serves on advisory committees in career and technical education at three area school districts. Passionate about education, he tells young people, "Never give up. Keep working hard, and keep a moral compass. Whatever you do, get involved with service and with your community."

Chronis's work in education was recognized by the Rio Grande Valley LEAD (Linking Economic and Academic Development), a partnership between education and business that prepares young people for the workforce, with the 2013 All Star Award. He received the award along with Dr. Cesar Maldonado, then president of TSTC Harlingen, and State Senator Eddie Lucio Jr. Chronis was also the speaker for TSTC Harlingen's spring 2013 commencement.

Recipients of the Rio Grande Valley LEAD 2013 All Star Award. Left to right: Dr. Cesar Maldonado, former president of the Harlingen campus; Albert Chronis; and State Senator Eddie Lucio Jr., District 27.

Albert Chronis addresses the 2013 graduating class at the Harlingen commencement.

Maria Acuna and Belinda Palomino

Although they attended Texas State Technical College (TSTC) at different campuses and more than twenty years apart, Maria Aguirre Acuna and Belinda Palomino have very similar stories. Both are first-generation college students, both pursued advanced degrees, both work today for the TSTC campuses they first attended, and both earned the title Miss TSTC in 1986 and 2009, respectively. The most impressive similarity, though, is their shared passion for TSTC and its students.

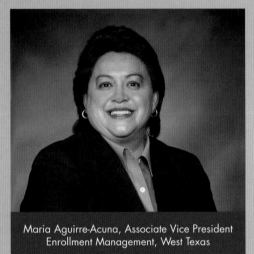

Maria Aguirre-Acuna, Associate Vice President Enrollment Management, West Texas

Now the associate vice president for enrollment management at TSTC West Texas, Acuna was introduced to the campus by then Assistant Manager Homer K. Taylor during a recruiting trip in her hometown of Del Rio. Explaining that Taylor has mentored her throughout her thirty years at TSTC, Acuna said he gave her a job as the night switchboard operator. "City Hall in Del Rio had a similar system, and I was familiar with it because of a high school co-op program. I went to school, worked nights, and studied at the switchboard." Acuna graduated with three associate's degrees and continued to work for the West Texas campus. She says, "I stayed at Texas State Technical College because of the lives we change."

Palomino received her core curriculum at TSTC Harlingen and went on to earn a bachelor's degree in communication studies from the University of Texas Pan American. "I wanted to go into broadcasting, but I found that I liked interacting with people and I enjoyed the analytics of communication." At TSTC, Palomino went from being very shy to becoming a strong student leader, including a year as student government president during which she had the opportunity to testify before the legislature on behalf of the school. "TSTC brought me out of my shell."

Note: In 1986, when Maria Aguirre Acuna received her crown, Texas State Technical College was still called Texas State Technical Institute. Consequently, Acuna's title was actually Miss TSTI.

The experience shifted her focus to student affairs. "My advisor at UT Pan American used to make fun of me because I was always talking about TSTC." When a job as supervisor of student activities became open at the Harlingen campus, it was natural for Palomino to apply. She has served in that position since August 2012.

Palomino's advice to students is "get involved." She believes TSTC is a great place to develop leadership skills and to pursue a career. "If two students are doing well academically, the difference [for an employer] may be whether one has a transcript which includes involvement in co-curricular activities." Involvement is something Palomino takes to heart, as evidenced by the Gold Level of the President's Volunteer Service Award she received in 2014 for 250 documented hours of community service.

Belinda Palomino, Supervisor Student Activities, Harlingen campus

Involvement is also important to Acuna. She serves on the executive board of the Texas Association of Chicanos in Higher Education as the vice president of communications, as well as on the executive board of the Texas Association of Collegiate Registrars and Admissions Officers. Acuna continued her education while working at TSTC. She earned a bachelor's degree in 2006 and a master's degree in 2011 from Wayland Baptist University in Lubbock.

As an admissions officer, she frequently advises students. "Students should take a good look at what they want to do, but technology is what continues to move the world around us. A technology degree can be a starting point to continued success. People can lose houses and cars, but a degree is something they will never lose."

Dan Garza

Raised in the lower Rio Grande Valley, Dan Garza grew up traveling in the summers to work in the fields picking vegetables and fruit. "My parents did not want the same life for me, and they knew education was the key." With few resources and little direction, Garza joined the US Air Force right out of high school. Four years later, with a wife and two small children, Garza enrolled in Texas State Technical Institute (TSTI) in Harlingen in the computer maintenance technology program. "TSTI was a door of opportunity for me. Other than [marrying] my wife, it was the most important step in my life."

Hired by 3M prior to graduation from TSTI in 1985, Garza now serves as the plant engineering manager for 3M's 816,000-square-foot Brownwood facility. He has since earned both a bachelor's and a master's degree.

Garza's introduction to 3M came through one of his instructors who arranged a trip to Austin for Garza and six other TSTI students. When the students traveled north for their interviews, 3M was still new to Austin. Most operations were located in leased buildings, as the industry giant had not yet built its 1,200,000-square-foot research and development facility in Austin. The trip and interviews were 3M's first introduction to TSTI, now Texas State Technical College (TSTC). Garza was the company's first hire from the school. Today, TSTC graduates comprise 33 percent of Garza's workforce.

Encouraged to do so by 3M, Garza has maintained his connection to TSTC by participating on numerous advisory committees and assisting with new program development on multiple campuses. "It is very important for employers to understand that they have a huge opportunity to impact the quality of graduates today. TSTC will respond, and has always responded without a lot of red tape, to what industry needs. In the advisory committee system, employers can have direct input and a real-time connection to the quality of new hires."

Dan Garza joined 3M right after graduation. He is now the plant engineering manager at 3M's Brownwood facility. (Courtesy of Dan Garza)

TSTC Graduate beats odds, climbs corporate ladder at 3M

Dan Garza grew up in a tiny South Texas village along the banks of the Rio Grande River.

"As a youth in Granjeno, you were respected for your street smarts, not for listening to teachers and opening books; you had to maintain your pride – you acted tough," Dan said.

Fortunately for Dan, along with maintaining a tough image, he also maintained a strong grade-point average. Math was his favorite subject, and he was a member of the National Honor Society at his school in Granjeno. Dan's parents and high school counselors pleaded with him to pursue a college education upon graduation, but to Dan they were just words – the things parents and teachers were supposed to say.

"I couldn't relate to the idea of going to college. My mother received a sixth grade education in Mexico, and my father received a third grade education in South Texas. They were both migrant farm workers. I had no Hispanic role models who attended college," Dan said.

Despite receiving acceptance letters from several colleges and a generous offer from General Motors of a full scholarship and a job upon graduation, Dan chose to join the Air Force.

At the same time Dan joined the Air Force, his cousin, just out of the Air Force, enrolled in Texas State Technical College at Harlingen. He became the role model Dan never had, and Dan followed his progress closely.

Eighteen months later, Dan's cousin graduated from TSTC Harlingen with an associate's degree in Computer Maintenance Technology. He landed a job with Dow Chemical Company in Shreveport making $2,400 a month. "This motivated me," Dan said. "I had never stepped foot on a TSTC campus, but I knew I wanted to go there."

In the fall of 1993, after four years in the Air Force, Dan enrolled in the Computer Maintenance Technology program at TSTC Harlingen.

"I knew it would be hard. I now had my wife and two kids to take care of," Dan said. "What

Dan Garza (r.) and Warren Johnson, Engineering Manager for 3M's Austin Center, talk with Vergil Belt, a TSTC Waco graduate and utility plant control room operator.

attracted me to TSTC was the fact that I could get an education in only two years and still get a job that paid well. I knew I wouldn't be able to take care of my family as well as I would like to for a couple of years, but I was determined to do well in school and secure a good job after graduation."

Ten years after graduating from Texas State Technical College, Dan has made outstanding progress at 3M and has reached another career plateau. In August 1994, he was promoted to plant engineering supervisor with responsibilities for four plant engineering departments. He is now earning a high salary and is a step closer to his goal of becoming a plant manager.

Throughout his career, Dan has maintained close ties with the Texas State Technical College System. He was instrumental in establishing two full 3M scholarships for high school students attending TSTC, and he serves on three TSTC Advisory Committees: the electronics core program at Harlingen, the metrology program at Amarillo, and the manufacturing technology program at Sweetwater.

"This year my wife and I celebrated our 15th wedding anniversary, and we have three beautiful children. I have a very comfortable life and a bright future for my family," Dan said. "When I talk to the youth in the community, I don't just tell them they should continue their education; I share with them a true story . . . my story. I'm very proud to state the fact that Texas State Technical College gave me a great start. It played a vital role in opening a big door of opportunity in my life – 3M – and the doors are still opening."

5

Lisa Torgerson

Headed to college on a tennis scholarship, Lisa Torgerson surprised her mother and abruptly switched course. She enrolled, instead, in the horticulture program at Texas State Technical Institute (TSTI). "The Waco campus was known for its horticulture degree. Back then, there was only one new building on campus. Everything was old and converted [from the former air force base originally located there], but what you learned was great. The facilities—they were not so great."

Torgerson started mowing yards when she was fifteen and found she loved it. "Women didn't do physical jobs then, and there wasn't a lawn maintenance industry. Even if there had been, women wouldn't have been in it, unless you count floral design." As a result, Torgerson's mother "thought it was absolutely ridiculous for me to continue to mow yards," but she grew to respect her daughter's career choice.

Torgerson, who earned her degree in 1980, began to build her business while still at TSTI. "I worked at a nursery selling plants and at Mr. Gattis selling pizza, and went to school." Torgerson, though, wanted to start mowing yards, so she sold her car and bought an old truck. She acquired some commercial clients and never looked back.

Torgerson has owned Lawns Ltd. in Waco since 1983. With a staff of forty to fifty employees, Lawns Ltd. is a full-service company providing design/build services in maintenance, landscape, irrigation, and lighting for residential and commercial properties. "When I started, no one did this professionally, but lawn service has morphed into a respected industry."

Torgerson, who hires graduates from Texas State Technical College (TSTC), believes in technical education. "Technical colleges like TSTC allow students to enter their career path faster than four-year schools, and they statistically have a higher job placement rate." Although Torgerson earned a teaching degree from Baylor in 1983, the second degree confirmed teaching was not to be her future. Torgerson advises students today to focus on their passion. "You are more likely to stay in your career if it is also your passion."

Lisa Torgerson, owns Lawns Ltd., a thriving outdoor services company in Waco, Texas. (Photo by Marlene S. McMichael)

Denise Jenson

Besides their family ties, the Jenson's also have Texas State Technical College (TSTC) in common. Three of them graduated from TSTC West Texas, and the fourth, Denise Jenson, works at the Breckenridge campus.

Denise's mother, Donna Jenson, earned a degree in software and business management in the early 1990s. Sister Dana Jenson Moser earned a certificate in health information technology in 2003, and brother Dusty Jenson earned a degree in environmental science technology (EST) in 2012. All three attended the Breckenridge campus, and all three have remained in West Texas working in their field of study.

In keeping with the family's TSTC tradition started by her mother, Denise Jenson now works as an admissions advisor and recruiter for TSTC, but she has plans to enroll in the EST program. "TSTC is a fantastic choice for a student. We offer in-demand programs for hot jobs, which allow you to stay in the community and work in a good career. We also require that you learn job-search skills and offer career services for life!"

Cory Blue

A 2005 graduate from the Marshall campus, Cory Blue earned dual degrees in industrial maintenance and engineering technology and as an industrial electrician technician. Blue currently works in Indonesia for Diamond Offshore Drilling Inc., maintaining the electronic equipment on a drilling rig. Blue plans to stay in the oil and gas industry and hopes eventually to move into management. "I get to spend six months out of the year with my children and still earn three times more than I could locally. Before, I worked two jobs at a time, making minimum wage. Technical school opened a door for me and paved the way for my future success."

Cory Blue enjoys extended time with family when not working on the oil rig. (Courtesy of Cory Blue)

Student

Life

Texas is enjoying a vibrant economy fueled by an expanding business sector. For this to continue, the state must have a workforce that is well trained and dependable. This is the role of Texas State Technical College—to supply and train that workforce.

Each of the nine, dedicated individuals on TSTC's Board of Regents has a key role in making and implementing policy that governs TSTC. Serving as their chairman has been one of the most rewarding endeavors I have ever undertaken. At TSTC, we change lives, and we ensure the state's vitality. To know that is a feeling that is hard to describe. I have said I would not trade this job for any other college or university chairmanship in Texas. Today, I feel stronger than ever about that.

Ellis M. Skinner II
Chairman
Texas State Technical College Board of Regents

John Henry "Jack" Kultgen, first chairman of the board of regents

Chapter 9
Excellence Through Leadership

The list of men and women who have served as regents for Texas State Technical College (TSTC) reads like a who's who of the most influential in Texas government and business over the last half century.

None, however, present a stronger personality or a more iconic image than TSTC's very first chairman of the board of regents, John Henry "Jack" Kultgen.

Kultgen's truest legacy rests in his public service after he gained business success. A native of Chicago, Kultgen found himself in Dallas in the 1920s selling automobiles. He moved his family to Waco in 1936 to become the managing partner of the local Ford dealership, now Bird-Kultgen Ford. By the mid-1940s, he was a recognized community leader.

Kultgen served on numerous local boards, usually with a stint as president or chairman. He was widely viewed as an organizer and fundraiser, chairing efforts to save both of the city's private hospitals, to revitalize the Roosevelt Hotel, to create Waco's United Fund, and to build Baylor University's Floyd Casey Stadium. He was also instrumental in Waco's relatively tranquil transition into desegregation in the early 1960s and in improving the education

and business practices of Paul Quinn College, an African Methodist Episcopal Church college, now relocated to Dallas.

White and Catholic, Kultgen was often queried about why he championed the causes he did. "When you can get people working together and helping each other, why, they don't have much prejudice left." Of the Baylor stadium project, he added, "I was interested in the city…It wouldn't have made any difference to me if it'd been a Methodist or Presbyterian or what it was. It was here, and it needed support." About his work in the African American community, Kultgen said, "I think that a lot of people wondered why I spent so much time trying to help them, but it seemed to me that it was the thing to do."

Kultgen's influence did not stop at the Waco city limits. Under five Texas governors, he served on some of the state's most powerful boards and commissions, including the Brazos River Authority and the Texas Highway Commission. Kultgen made more than forty trips to Washington, DC, to secure funding for the Waco Dam and other flood control dams in the Brazos River basin. At the time, Kultgen called the Waco Dam "the biggest single factor in the progress of Waco in the last hundred years." Additionally, even before his tenure on the highway commission, Kultgen brokered the deal which allowed Interstate 35 to be built through Waco, instead of around the city as the federal government intended.

As part of the three-member citizens' group tasked with finding a new use for the James Connally Air Force Base, Kultgen was obviously very involved in TSTC's birth in Waco. His influence, however, could be felt on every campus. Following his 1969 appointment to the board of regents by Governor Preston Smith, Kultgen crisscrossed the country, negotiating terms with the federal government and the US Air Force for the air force bases which became new campus locations. He was everywhere—at campus ribbon-cutting ceremonies, before the legislature asking for funding, and in front of community leaders.

Of his role as the first chairman of the board of regents, Kultgen called himself "an obvious victim" because of his involvement with the school from its inception. He and the other regents soon realized that Texas industry's need for trained workers exceeded their original understanding. Multiple jobs waited for every TSTC graduate.

"We had no idea of getting people degrees; we had no idea of turning out scholars; we had no idea of a four-year school or three-year school. Our idea was to take them [students] in and improve their skills or provide them with skills so that, when they got through, they could make a living. That's the only—that was really the objective of the whole school."

It is a vision which remains TSTC's primary objective today—skilled workers for real jobs.

The J. H. Kultgen Automotive Technology Center, the first new building on the Waco campus, was refurbished in 2014. (Photo by Marlene S. McMichael)

Gail and Jere Lawrence

It is somehow appropriate that a simple classified ad in the *St. Louis Post-Dispatch* precipitated Gail Robinson Lawrence's life-altering decision to leave her family in northern Illinois in 1984 for a state 1,100 miles away. Taught from an early age that there was nothing she could not do, Lawrence had never been afraid to take the road less traveled, as evidenced by her devotion to competitive swimming despite the fact that her school did not have a girls' program. She simply practiced with the boys' team.

Gail Lawrence
Vice Chancellor

Still, she surprised even her parents when she accepted a position in human resources with Hendrick Health System in Abilene, Texas—where she had no friends and no ties to home. A chance encounter on move-in day, however, led to a blind date with her future husband, Kyle Lawrence, and ensured Texas remained her permanent home.

The Lawrence family has deep roots in West Texas and a double connection to Texas State Technical College (TSTC). Jere Lawrence, Gail Lawrence's father-in-law, served on the TSTC Board of Regents from 1995 through 2003. Gail Lawrence has served in numerous positions, starting in 2002 as director of human resources of TSTC West Texas and moving up to president of the multi-campus college. She now serves TSTC at the system level as vice chancellor for corporate relations.

The commitment to duty and to public service has defined both the Lawrence family and Gail Lawrence's career. For example, three generations of Lawrence men have served as mayor of Sweetwater. Jere Lawrence served on the boards of two additional universities while serving on the TSTC Board of Regents. In addition, he served on the boards of several state and national professional organizations, including multiple terms as chairman.

Gail Lawrence, however, prefers to work behind the scenes. As a result, the decision to accept a promotion to president of TSTC West Texas was a difficult one. "The pulse [of the campus] is not in the president's office. It is with the students."

Students are Gail Lawrence's constant focus. "If you are not careful, you can lock yourself away doing important things as an administrator." In

order to ensure she understood the issues firsthand, Lawrence moved herself out of the administrative offices and into the nursing building when she was tasked with saving the troubled nursing program at TSTC West Texas a few years ago. With a background in health care, she knew that losing the program would be devastating for the region.

Jere Lawrence, Board of Regents (1995–2003) and Chairman (1997–2001)

By 2012, the nursing program at TSTC West Texas realized a 100 percent pass rate in its state-administered exit exams, known as the National Council Licensure Examination for Registered Nurses (NCLEX-RN) and the highest starting salaries of any two-year registered nursing program in Texas, according to the Texas Workforce Commission.

Lawrence approached the college's declining enrollment the same way—she talked to employers, specifically those in the oil and gas industry. The result was a fifteen-week program to train downhole tool technicians, who earn starting salaries of $45,000 to $60,000 in addition to benefits. The program, along with other changes made under Gail Lawrence's leadership, generated the highest percentage of enrollment growth at TSTC West Texas of any two-year institution in the fall of 2013, according to the Texas Higher Education Coordinating Board.

Lawrence served as only the second female president of a TSTC campus. She uses the collaborative, problem-solving approaches she perfected as president in her new role in corporate relations for TSTC's eleven locations. Her goal is to reach out to industry in order to match TSTC programs and students with real jobs. According to Lawrence, "Seeing whole families change because of one graduate is profound."

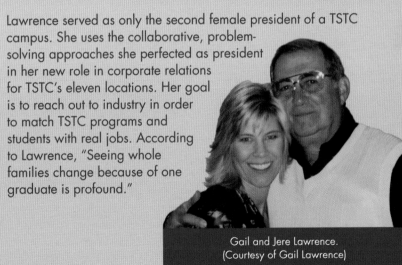

Gail and Jere Lawrence.
(Courtesy of Gail Lawrence)

Board of Directors

Texas A&M University

James Connally Technical Institute 1965–1969

A. P. Beutel

Wofford Cain

Sterling C. Evans

H. C. Heldenfels

Peyton McKnight Jr.

J. W. Newton (term ended 1966)

L. F. Peterson

Gardiner Symonds

Clyde Thompson (term ended 1968)

Clyde H. Wells

S. B. Whittenburg

Board of Regents Chairmen

Texas State Technical Institute, 1969–1991

Texas State Technical College, 1991–Present

Name	Board Term	Chairman Term
J. H. Kultgen	1969–1980	1969–1980
William M. Streckert	1971–1984	1980–1982
Liborio Hinojosa	1979–1985	1982–1984
Ralph Lowenfield	1979–1985	1984–1985
H. Gene Evans	1984–1987	1985–1987
F. Herman Coleman	1980–1987	1987–1987
Ed Aiken Jr.	1984–1989	1988–1989
George Fred Rhodes	1985–1991	1989–1991
George W. Baur	1987–1993	1992–1993
Jere Ruff	1987–1995	1993–1995
Edward B. Adams Sr.	1992–1997	1995–1997
Jere Lawrence	1995–2003	1997–2001
Bernie Francis	1997–2003	2001–2004
Connie de la Garza	1995–2007	2004–2007
J. V. Martin	2004–2015	2008–2010
Dr. Rolf R. Haberecht	2006–2011	2010–2011
Michael F. Northcutt	2002–2013	2011–2012
Ellis M. Skinner II	2009–2019	2012–2015

Board of Directors

The Texas A&M University System

Board of Regents Members

Texas State Technical Institute, 1969–1991

Texas State Technical College, 1991–Present

Francis V. Wallace	1969–1971	David W. Taylor	1990–1991
Harold G. Tate	1969–1971	Richard Gutierrez	1990–1995
Henry C. Schulte	1969–1973	Gerald D. Phariss	1992–1997
Joe J. Garza	1969–1979	Odelia M. Reyna McEachern	1992–1995
John W. Nigliazzo	1969–1975	Charles D. Olson	1994–1999
Richard Thomas	1969–1973	Nat Lopez	1994–1999
Russel B. Watson Jr.	1969–1971	Tom L. Ragland	1994–1999
Yancey Price	1969–1975	Dr. Jerilyn K. Pfeifer	1995–2007
Charles E. Wright Sr.	1971–1984	Thomas L. Whaley Sr.	1995–2001
Morris E. Bailey	1971–1973	Amy Tschirhart	1997–2002
Lance Sears	1973–1978	Linda Routh	1999–2005
Oscar D. Seastrunk	1973–1979	Peterson Foster	1999–2001
T. D. Steinke	1973–1981	Terry Preuninger	1999–2005
Tom Patterson	1973–1979	Barbara Rusling	2002–2009
T. J. Richards	1975–1981	Don Elliot	2002–2005
H. W. Monzingo	1978–1984	Nora Castaneda	2004–2009
Jesse S. Harris	1979–1985	Joe K. Hearne	2006–2017
James A. Besselman	1981–1987	Joe M. Gurecky	2006–2017
Ralph T. Dosher Jr.	1981–1987	Gene Seaman	2008–2013
Gerald D. Phariss	1984–1989	Linda McKenna	2009–2015
Dr. E. A. Aguilar	1985–1991	Penny Forrest	2009–2015
Mollie Anna Solomon	1985–1995	John Hatchel	2011–2017
Jesse S. Harris	1987–1993	Ivan Andarza	2013–2019
John E. Davis	1988–1993	Keith Honey	2013–2019
Noe Fernandez	1989–1990		

James Connally Technical Institute of Texas A&M University, 1965–1969
Texas State Technical Institute, 1969–1991
Texas State Technical College, 1991–Present

Leader	Role	Organization	Tenure
Dr. Roy W. Dugger	Director	JCTI	1965–1969
	President	TSTI	1969–1974
	President Emeritus	TSTI	1974–1976
Dr. Maurice W. Roney	President	TSTI	1974–1979
Dr. Jack E. Tompkins	Acting President	TSTI	1979–1980
	President	TSTI	1980–1987
Dr. James A. Bird	Acting President	TSTI	1987–1988
Dr. Donald G. Garrison	Chancellor	TSTI	1988
Dr. James A. Bird	Acting Chancellor	TSTI	1988–1989
Dr. Cecil L. Groves	Chancellor	TSTI	1989–1991
	Chancellor	TSTC	1991–1996
Ralph L. Strother	Interim Chancellor	TSTC	1996–1997
Dr. Bill Segura	Chancellor	TSTC	1998–2010
Michael L. Reeser	Chancellor	TSTC	2010–Present

James Connally Technical Institute of Texas A&M University, 1965–1969
Texas State Technical Institute – James Connally Campus, 1969–1991
Texas State Technical College Waco, 1991–Present

Leader	Role	Organization	Tenure
Dr. Roy W. Dugger	Vice President Director	TAMU JCTI	 1965–1969
Dr. Jack E. Tompkins	Acting General Manager	James Connally Campus	1970–1974
Dr. Robert D. Krienke	General Manager President	James Connally Campus TSTI Waco	1974–1983 1983–1988
Donald E. Goodwin	President	TSTI Waco TSTC Waco	1989–1991 1991–1994
Dr. Fred L. Williams	President	TSTC Waco	1995–1999
Elton E. Stuckly Jr.	Interim President	TSTC Waco	1999
Dr. Martha M. Ellis	President	TSTC Waco	2000–2002
Elton E. Stuckly Jr.	Interim President	TSTC Waco	2002
Dr. Brent Knight	President	TSTC Waco	2002
Dr. Elton E. Stuckly Jr.	Interim President President	TSTC Waco TSTC Waco	2002 2003–2014
Rob Wolaver	Interim President	TSTC Waco	2014–Present

Texas State Technical College Waco

Texas State Technical Institute – Rolling Plains Campus, 1970–1978
Texas State Technical Institute Sweetwater, 1978–1991
Texas State Technical College Sweetwater, 1991–2011
Texas State Technical College West Texas, 2011–Present

Leader	Role	Organization	Tenure
D. A. Pevehouse	General Manager	Rolling Plains Campus	1970–1978
		TSTI Sweetwater	1978–1981
Dr. Hebert C. Robbins	General Manager	TSTI Sweetwater	1982–1983
	President	TSTI Sweetwater	1983–1987
Dr. Clay Johnson	President	TSTI Sweetwater	1987–1991
	President	TSTC Sweetwater	1991–1998
Homer K. Taylor	President	TSTC Sweetwater	1999–2004
Michael L. Reeser	President	TSTC Sweetwater	2004–2010
Gail Lawrence	President	TSTC Sweetwater	2010–2011
	President	TSTC West Texas	2011–2013
Kyle Smith	Interim President	TSTC West Texas	2013–Present

(Photo by Marlene S. McMichael)

Texas State Technical Institute – Mid-Continent Campus, 1970–1978
Texas State Technical Institute Amarillo, 1978–1991
Texas State Technical College Amarillo, 1991–1995

Leader	Role	Organization	Tenure
Colonel Hill W. Beasley	Vice President	Mid-Continent Campus	1969–1970
Dr. Jasper N. Baker	General Manager	Mid-Continent Campus	1970–1973
Lovell A. Pillow	General Manager	Mid-Continent Campus	1973–1978
Dr. James A. Bird	General Manager	TSTI Amarillo	1978–1982
Ronald L. DeSpain	General Manager President	TSTI Amarillo TSTI Amarillo TSTC Amarillo	1982–1991 1991–1995
Ronald E. Abrams	President	TSTC Amarillo	1995

Amarillo campus separated from TSTI in 1995 to become a part of Amarillo College.

Texas State Technical Institute – Rio Grande Campus, 1970–1983
Texas State Technical Institute Harlingen, 1983–1991
Texas State Technical College Harlingen, 1991–Present

Leader	Role	Organization	Tenure
Dr. Milton J. Schiller	Vice President	Rio Grande Campus	1970–1971
Archie Rosales	General Manager	Rio Grande Campus	1972–1978
Dr. J. Gilbert Leal	General Manager	Rio Grande Campus	1978–1983
	President	TSTI Harlingen	1983–1991
	President	TSTC Harlingen	1991–2008
Pat Hobbs	Interim President	TSTC Harlingen	2008
Dr. Cesar Maldonado	President	TSTC Harlingen	2008–2014
Dr. Stella Garcia	Interim President	TSTC Harlingen	2014–Present

Texas State Technical College Harlingen

Texas State Technical College Marshall, 1999–Present

Leader	Role	Organization	Tenure
Dr. Joe A. Green	President	TSTC Marshall	1999–2002
Dr. J. Gary Hendricks	President	TSTC Marshall	2002–2007
Colonel Randall Wooten	President	TSTC Marshall	2007–2014
Bart Day	Provost	TSTC Marshall	2014–Present

Texas State Technical College Marshall

The Ongoing Connally Connection

Research for this book revealed a previously unknown familial link between Colonel James T. Connally and Governor John B. Connally. Administrators had always assumed the two Connallys were not related. The family connection came to light through another Connally, also one in public service. Luke A. P. Connally, a veteran of Iraq and the US Marine Corps, currently serves as the field representative for Congressman Bill Flores (TX-17), whose district includes the Waco campus at which the two earlier Connallys played such significant roles. Colonel Connally and Governor Connally were fourth cousins. In 2012, Luke Connally received his commercial aircraft pilot training with instrument rating in the facility named after the colonel. He and the colonel are third cousins twice removed. He and the governor are fourth cousins twice removed.

(Photo by Marlene S. McMichael)

The younger Connally recently accepted a position with Alaska Missions as assistant chief of operations, where his duties will include creating and organizing retreats for formerly deployed soldiers and their families with a focus on healing and restoration. He and his family will join Alaska Missions in Anchorage in the summer of 2015.

The three Connallys share an impressive legacy of service to Texas and their country, a legacy which includes Texas State Technical College.

Friends:

We all have a story to tell about Texas State Technical College (TSTC). For me, that story includes three family members who are TSTC graduates. Raised in the Waco area, I would have also gone to TSTC, except that my curve ball landed me somewhere else for a time. When I joined TSTC's administrative staff in 2013, in many ways, I was just coming home.

In doing so, I learned, again, the depth to which TSTC changes students' lives. I hope this book, *Texas State Technical College: The Vision, The Leaders, The Heart,* has inspired you as it has unfolded the TSTC story. More importantly, I hope it has birthed a desire in you to participate in that story. It would be difficult to find an institution more important to the Texas economy than TSTC.

In 2015, we celebrate TSTC's rich heritage. We honor all those who have invested their talents and resources in this institution. We revel in our students' successes. Most importantly, we anticipate a bright future and vibrant economy fueled by an available, highly skilled workforce.

My job is to help build relationships with those from TSTC's past and present to secure that future. Together, we can build a "culture of philanthropy" strong enough to support TSTC for the next fifty years. Now more than ever, the growing demand for technically competent workers means TSTC's investor base must also grow. TSTC changes lives, and TSTC builds a stronger Texas. It has done so for fifty years. We are counting on you to help us as we engage for the next fifty.

How?

The TSTC Foundation is our gathering place—where friends, alumni, and industry representatives gather to support and advocate for TSTC. Become a member of the TSTC Foundation. Invest in TSTC's future.

Together, let us celebrate our history and prepare for fifty more years.

Jeff L. Kilgore
Vice Chancellor and Chief Marketing Officer/CEO of TSTC Foundation
www.tstcfoundation.org

Bibliography

Aguirre Acuna, Maria. Telephone interview, February 11, 2014.

Allen, James. Telephone interview, March 4, 2014.

An Act relating to authorizing the Board of Directors of Texas A&M University to accept James Connally Air Force Base on behalf of the State of Texas and to establish thereon the James Connally Technical Institute of Texas A&M University offering vocational and vocational-technical education programs. S.B. 487, 59th Legislature (1965). Legislative Reference Library of Texas.

An Act relating to creating and establishing in Amarillo, Potter County, Texas, a coeducational institute of vocational and vocational-technical education to be known as Amarillo Technical Institute of Texas A&M University. H.B. 66, 61st Legislature (1969). Legislative Reference Library of Texas.

An Act relating to changing the name of James Connally Technical Institute of Texas A&M University to the Texas State Technical Institute; providing an effective date. H.B. 137, 61st Legislature (1969). Legislative Reference Library of Texas.

An Act relating to authorizing a campus of Texas State Technical Institute in Nolan County. H.B. 672, 61st Legislature (1969). Legislative Reference Library of Texas.

An Act appropriating state funds to the Texas State Technical Institute for constructing and equipping an instructional building. S.B. 67, 64th Legislature (1975). Legislative Reference Library of Texas.

An Act relating to vocational and technical training programs provided by the Texas State Technical Institute. H.B. 178, 68th Legislature (1983). Legislative Reference Library of Texas.

An Act relating to postsecondary technical-vocational education, to Texas State Technical Institute, and to certain powers and duties of the coordinating board; creating a joint advisory committee. S.B. 911, 69th Legislature (1985). Legislative Reference Library of Texas.

An Act relating to funding for the Texas State Technical Institute and extension programs operated by the institute. S.B. 1028, 71st Legislature (1989). Legislative Reference Library of Texas.

An Act relating to the Texas State Technical College System, its organization, duties, and powers, including that of eminent domain and the authority to issue bonds. S.B. 1222, 72nd Legislature (1991). Legislative Reference Library of Texas.

An Act relating to the establishment of an extension center of Texas State Technical Institute in the city of Marshall in Harrison County. S.B. 1357, 72nd Legislature (1991). Legislative Reference Library of Texas.

An Act relating to the conversion of the McAllen extension center of Texas State Technical College to a joint-county junior college. S.B. 251, 73rd Legislature (1993). Legislative Reference Library of Texas.

An Act relating to the lease of the Amarillo campus of the Texas State Technical College System to Amarillo College. H.B. 2507, 74th Legislature (1995). Legislative Reference Library of Texas.

An Act relating to designating the Texas State Technical College System extension center in the city of Marshall as a campus of the system. H.B. 1049, 76th Legislature (1999). Legislative Reference Library of Texas.

An Act relating to the creation of the East Williamson County Multi-Institution Teaching Center. H.B. 2074, 80th Legislature (2007). Legislative Reference Library of Texas.

An Act relating to the degrees awarded by the Texas State Technical College System. H.B. 1325, 81st Legislature (2009). Legislative Reference Library of Texas.

An Act relating to the Texas State Technical College System. S.B. 489, 82nd Legislature (2011). Legislative Reference Library of Texas.

Arellano Jr., Gregoria. Telephone interview, February 11, 2014.

Avery, Charles N. Personal letter to Irene K. Walton, November 5, 2010.

Avery, Charles N. Personal interview, August 9, 2013.

Baylor Institute for Oral History, Thomas Lee Charlton interview of Betty June Neese Barkley on July 29, 1983, and March 28, 1985. Print.

Baylor Institute for Oral History, Thomas Lee Charlton interview of Dr. Roy Wesley Dugger on June 8, 21, and 29, 1982. Print.

Baylor Institute for Oral History, Thomas Lee Charlton interview of J. H. Kultgen on June 27 and July 16, 1974. Print.

Baylor Institute for Oral History, Volume 1, Thomas Lee Charlton interview of William Robert "Bob" Poage. 1971-79. Print.

Baylor News 11. "To infinity and beyond." no. 6 (2001): 7.

Belcher, Zack. "Press Release: James Connally Technical Institute." *JCTI*, n.d.

Blue, Cory. Telephone interview, February 18, 2014.

Brownwood News. "Enrollment up More Than 23% at TSTC West Texas." September 17, 2013. Accessed December 28, 2013. http://www.brownwoodnews.com/index.php?option=com_content&view=article&id=13140:enrollment-up-more-than-23-at-tstc-west-texas-&catid=37:business&Itemid=60.

Chavez, Dominic. "THECB Releases Preliminary 2013 Enrollment Data for Higher Education." *Texas Higher Education Coordinating Board*. October 24, 2013.

Chronis, Albert G. Telephone interview, February 4, 2014.

Clark, Samantha. Telephone interview, February 10, 2014.

Connally/Harlingen Navigators & Observers. www.james-connally.org.

Copeland, Mike. "Waco civic leader David Kultgen dies." *Waco Tribune-Herald*, May 20, 2013. Accessed February 28, 2014. http://www.wacotrib.com/news/greater_waco/waco-civic-leader-david-kultgen-dies/article_f2d42c40-e09f-5692-b7b8-d067ab33ba7e.html.

Essex, Allen. "Harlingen Army Airfield: School for TOP GUNS." *Valley Morning Star*, May 22, 2009. Accessed October 2, 2014. http://www.valleymorningstar.com/news/article_5c51c334-f281-5813-b380-b17491cd1421.html?mode=image&photo=1Texas State Technical Institute

Garza, Dan. Telephone interview, March 6, 2014.

Get Connected. "New Student Orientation 2011-2012."

Gordon, Joe. "TSTI Offices Are Opened." *Sweetwater Reporter*, July 9, 1970, p. 1.

Gyure, Joseph. "Interstate 35 dramatically changed Waco's face." Waco History Project. September 29, 1950. Accessed February 28, 2014. www.wacohistoryproject.ort/places/i35.html.

Hamilton, Reeve. "Technical College Faces Questions and a Paradigm Shift." *Texas Tribune*. Accessed December 28, 2013. www.texastribune.org/2013/07/28/questions-and-paradigm-shift-technical-college/.

History, Texas State Technical Institute, 1971.

Horn, Jeff. Telephone interview, February 14, 2014.

Jenson, Denise. Telephone interview, February 18, 2014.

Karl, Heather. Presentation made at TSTC Leadership Institute, March 2014.

KTXS. "TSTC West Texas sees significant enrollment increase." August 28, 2013. Accessed December 28, 2013. http://www.ktxs.com/news/tstc-west-texas-sees-significant-enrollment-increase/21687306.

Lawrence, Gail. Telephone interview, December 20, 2013.

Leal, Gilbert. Telephone interview, May 24, 2014.

Lovelace, Bob. Telephone interview, September 26, 2014.

McMahan, Robb. Telephone interview, February 17, 2014.

National WASP Museum. www.waspmuseum.org.

Norman, Amanda. Baylor University. Accessed February 6, 2014. www.blogs.baylor.edu/texascollection/2012/09/14/a-fittin-home-for-the-fightin-baylor-bears-the1949-1950-stadium-campaign/.

Palomino, Belinda. Telephone interview, February 7, 2014.

Perkins, Scheherazade. Telephone interview, February 3, 2014.

Perry, Dick. "Stadium Is Realized Dream." *Daily Lariat*. September 29, 1950, p. 1.

Plantier, Keith. Telephone interview, February 7, 2014.

Provence, Harry. "From James Connally AFB to Texas State Technical College." Waco History Project. Accessed December 8, 2013. www.wacohistoryproject.org/firstperson/harryprovence.html.

Reeser, Michael. Telephone interview, March 10, 2014.

Reeser, Michael. "Paradigm Shift: The Age of Mass Customization - Part 1." *TSTC Magazine*, Fall 2013, 14.

———. "Paradigm Shift: The Age of Mass Customization - Part 2." *TSTC Magazine*, Spring 2014, 13.

Romig, Bruce. "January Opening Planned for Vocational Institute." *Amarillo Globe Times*. September 23, 1969.

———. "Selected at Waco." *Amarillo Globe Times*. September 22, 1969.

Segura, Bill. Telephone interview, March 4, 2014.

Sepulveda, Sam. Telephone interview, February 4, 2014.

Skinner, Ellis, II. Telephone interview, May 5, 2014.

Smith Welch, Karen. "Albertson's sells Amarillo store as part of United Supermarket's deal." *Amarillo Globe News*, December 2013. Accessed December 7, 2013. www.amarillo.com/news/local-news/2013-12-17.

Southern Association of Colleges and Schools Commission on Colleges. www.sacscoc.org.

Sowell, Greg. Telephone interview, January 28, 2014.

State of Texas Legislative Reference Library. Accessed January 6, 2014. www.lrl.state.tx.us.

Stuckly, Elton E. Personal interview, December 13, 2013.

Taylor, Homer K. Personal interview, November 4, 2013.

Tech Times Staff. "Dedication marks new era of TSTC aerospace history." Texas State Technical College. Accessed January 31, 2014. http://www.tstctechtimes.com/dedication-marks-new-era-of-tstc-aerospace-history-1.2875420.

Texas A&M University. "Board of Directors Meeting Minutes." May 21, 1965.

Texas State Historical Association. www.tshaonline.org.

———. Accessed October 8, 2013. http://www.tshaonline.org/handbook/online/articles/qbh01.

———. "William Robert Poage." May 21, 1965. Accessed November 23, 2013. http://www.tshaonline.org/handbook/online/articles/fpo50.

———. Accessed October 9, 2013. https://www.tshaonline.org/handbook/online/articles/qbj01.

———. Accessed October 9, 2013. http://www.tshaonline.org/handbook/online/articles/qba01.

———. Accessed October 9, 2013. http://www.tshaonline.org/handbook/online/articles/qcs01.

Texas State Technical College. 2014. www.tstc.edu.

———. "Board of Regents Meeting Minutes - 1969-2014."

———. "Dedication marks new era of TSTC aerospace history." Accessed December 2, 2013. www.tstctechtimes.com/dedication-marks-new-era-of-tstc-aerospace-history.

Texas State Technical Institute. *Texas State Technical Institute History*. Vol. 1. Waco, TX: TSTI, 1971.

Texas Technical Society Journal 1, no. 1 (October 1970): 1-16.

Torgerson, Lisa. Telephone interview, February 3, 2014.

TSTConnections. "TSTC among U.S. leaders producing Hispanic graduates." II, no. 1 (September 1993): 1.

TSTC Techline. "Harlingen campus serves as Valley site for 'Capital for a Day'." 1994.

"TSTI Annual Report 1981-82."

TSTI Development Foundation, Inc. "The Silver Anniversary of Texas State Technical Institute 1965-1990."

Waco News Tribune. "Dr. Roney No. 2 Man at TSTI." September 24, 1969.

———. "Salter Take Job With Firm on TSTI Campus." September 25, 1969, p. 11-A.

Waco Times-Herald. "State Tech's Regents O.K. Land Lease." January 20, 1970.

———. "Governor Asks State Take JCAFB For Top Level Technical School." April 5, 1965, p. 1.

Waco Tribune Herald. "Connally Tech Plans to Offer Truck Program." August 1, 1969, p. 10-A.

———. "Connally Tech Students To Begin Registration." August 31, 1969, p. 8-A.

———. "400 Acres Near JCTI Purchased as Industrial, Commercial Site." February 1, 1969, sec. 1-B.

———. "James Connally Airport Soon Opening to Public." August 29, 1969.

———. "Outstanding Citizen - All Seats Reserved for Award to Dugger." September 22, 1968.

———. "Pilot Program Registration at Connally." August 31, 1969, p. 8-A.

———. "School Research New Institute Founded Here." September 11, 1968.

Waco Tribune-Herald. "Bill Introduced to Turn Control of TSTI Campuses to Local Boards." March 11, 1971, p. 1.

———. "Conference Will Hear TSTI's Webb." March 25, 1971.

———. "Connally Tech Add 24 Teachers to Staff." October 19, 1969.

———. "New Bowling Alley Opens at Connally." October 30, 1970.

———. "New East Texas TSTI Site Sought by Solon." March 11, 1971.

———. "Prof Get New Post at TSTI." February 6, 1970.

———. "Regents of TSTI To Meet Monday." May 17, 1970.

———. "Smith Approves Buying of TSTI Campus Land." February 6, 1970.

———. "Smith Approves Rio Grande TSTI Campus Deed Transferal to Texas." March 10, 1971.

———. "Technical-Vocational Workshop Scheduled." June 6, 1970.

———. "TSTI Announces New Administrative Changes." May 19, 1970.

———. "TSTI Authorizes Dormitory Plan." November 23, 1971.

———. "TSTI Board of Regents Set Meeting for Monday." October 18, 1969.

———. "TSTI Breaks School Blood Donation Goal." October 23, 1970.

———. "TSTI Gets Debt-Service Dorm Grant." August 25, 1971.

———. "TSTI Holds Registration Next Week." August 28, 1971.

———. "TSTI Regents Approve Lease." May 19, 1970.

———. "TSTI Regents Meet." November 23, 1971.

———. "TSTI Students Attend 3M Clinic." October 16, 1970.

———. "TSTI Will Complete Purchase of Air Base." May 30, 1970.

———. "Vocational Workshop Opens June 8." June 6, 1970.

———. "Welding Seminar Set at TSTI." February 16, 1971.

———. "Workers Busy at TSTI, Quinn, MCC and Baylor." March 24, 1971.

Ward, Joe L. Jr. "Quiet desegregation of Waco's public facilities." Waco History Project. September 29, 1950. Accessed November 19, 2013. www.wacohistoryproject.org/firstperson/joeward.html.

Ware, Connie. Telephone interview, May 24, 2014.

Washington Monthly. "2013 Community College Rankings." Accessed January 31, 2014. www.washtingtonmonthly.com/college_guide/rankings_2013/community_rank.php.

Watson, Murray. Telephone interview, May 28, 2014.

Weatherall, Sami. Telephone interview, February 11, 2014.

Widup, Ron. Telephone interview, February 10, 2014.

Williams, Tony. Telephone interview, May 24, 2014.

Yeats, E. L., and Hooper Shelton. *History of Nolan County Texas*. Sweetwater, TX: Shelton Press, 1975.

About the Author

Marlene S. McMichael is a native Texan and has spent much of her career working in and around the Texas Legislature. She has held senior positions with five members of the Texas House of Representatives and a state senator. For nearly seven years, she was also executive director of the largest bipartisan caucus in the Texas Legislature, then widely recognized as the most influential group within the Texas House. During a sojourn from state government, McMichael worked for several private entities and eventually opened her own consulting firm, specializing in governmental affairs and community relations.

McMichael is currently associate vice chancellor for government affairs at Texas State Technical College and was a recipient of the Chancellor's Excellence Award in 2014. She is a summa cum laude graduate of Texas State University and the William P. Hobby Center for Public Service. McMichael holds a national certification as a Certified Public Manager®.

McMichael asserts that her greatest accomplishment is and always will be her daughter, Chara Anne McMichael. Together, they share a love for public service. The younger McMichael lives in Washington, DC, and serves as chief of staff for a Texas congressman. McMichael lives in Georgetown, Texas, where she remains active in her community and serves on a number of non-profit boards in Austin, Georgetown, and Killeen.